PURPOSEFUL

PURPOSEFUL

Are You a Manager
or a Movement Starter?

JENNIFER DULSKI

PORTFOLIO / PENGUIN

Portfolio/Penguin
An imprint of Penguin Random House LLC
375 Hudson Street
New York, New York 10014

Most Portfolio books are available at a discount when purchased in quantity for sales promotions or corporate use. Special editions, which include personalized covers, excerpts, and corporate imprints, can be created when purchased in large quantities. For more information, please call (212) 572-2232 or e-mail specialmarkets@penguinrandomhouse .com. Your local bookstore can also assist with discounted bulk purchases using the Penguin Random House corporate Business-to-Business program. For assistance in locating a participating retailer, e-mail B2B@penguinrandomhouse.com.

ISBN: 9780525536444 (export edition)

Library of Congress Cataloging-in-Publication Data

Names: Dulski, Jennifer, author.
Title: Purposeful : are you a manager or a movement starter? / Jennifer Dulski.
Description: New York : Portfolio/Penguin, [2018] |
Includes bibliographical references and index.
Identifiers: LCCN 2017050229| ISBN 9780735211377 (hardcover) |
ISBN 9780735211384 (epub)
Subjects: LCSH: Leadership. | Self-perception. | Perception. |
Social movements. | Executives.
Classification: LCC HD57.7 .D837 2018 | DDC 658.4/092—dc23
LC record available at https://lccn.loc.gov/2017050229

Printed in the United States of America
1   3   5   7   9   10   8   6   4   2

Book design by Tiffany Estreicher

For RED, EGD, and my other Enny

CONTENTS

CONTENTS

PURPOSEFUL

1

BE PURPOSEFUL

Defining movements

Anyone who thinks that they are too small to make a difference has never tried to fall asleep with a mosquito in the room.

—Christine Todd Whitman

THIS BOOK IS about how ordinary people make extraordinary change. It's not about politicians or CEOs of large companies who are already bestowed with enormous power and responsibility. It's about how your teammates, your neighbors, and you yourself can mobilize the people around you to bring your visions to life. So how does that happen?

• • •

FIVE MINUTES AFTER nineteen-year-old Manal Rostom switched seats with her cousin on a bus from Cairo to the Red Sea, the bus blew a tire and swerved into the desert, rolling over three times. Manal was okay, but her cousin, Mohammed, was instantly paralyzed. He died three weeks later. This shook Manal to her core. Her faith helped her cope with her grief and trauma, and though she had been only moderately religious before the accident, the experience strengthened her relationship to Islam. Two years later, although it wasn't necessarily expected by her family, Manal decided to wear the hijab, a traditional Muslim head covering. "It was a way to say thank you to God," she told me, "for giving me a second chance to live."

Manal wore the hijab for the next fourteen years. While she faced some criticism from Westerners who were either unfamiliar with the hijab or believe it is oppressive to women, she generally felt accepted in Egypt and Kuwait. And then something changed. More and more women she knew stopped wearing the hijab, anti-hijab articles started appearing in the media, and in Dubai, where she lived, Muslim women in hijab faced criticism and were not allowed into some public spaces. Manal didn't judge others negatively for choosing not to wear the hijab, but she felt that for herself and many other women, wearing the hijab provided a sense of connection to their faith. "I had a moment of epiphany," she said. "If I was to give in and just follow the crowd, then how would anything change? I felt like a dead fish who was just going to 'go with the flow,' but then I decided I wanted to go against the current. I wasn't a dead fish."

In 2014, Manal started a community of women to support each other through a group on Facebook called "Surviving Hijab," a name she chose because that's what she felt she was trying to do. That night in April, she invited eighty women, mainly her friends and family, into the group. When she woke up, she found that the group already had five hundred members. Within months, the community had grown to more than forty thousand women who supported and encouraged one another to be proud of wearing the hijab. Today, just three years later, Surviving Hijab is nearing five hundred thousand women from around the world and clearly fills a need for hijabi women to have a supportive community. Manal's desire to take action has created a movement.

With so many supporters behind her, Manal knew that more was possible. In addition to her job at a pharmaceutical company and her role leading this community, Manal is also an athlete—an avid runner. She faces even more criticism as a hijabi athlete, with people constantly asking her things like, "Won't you be hot running in all those layers?" She is often the only hijabi runner in races she competes in, and has seen it as an opportunity to help reduce stereotypes of Muslim women. But she wanted to do more. On the recommendation of a friend, and with the support of all the women in Surviving Hijab behind her, Manal wrote a letter to Tom Woolf, the head coach for Nike in the Middle East, titled "Nike Middle East— Veiled Women Runners :)" In it, she described her community of women and how she wanted to empower them to be active and do sports, even in the hijab. "The reason why I'm contacting you is because I have noticed that all pics featuring the Nike Club runners have no veiled women in them!" she wrote. "It's the Middle East, shouldn't we have some?" When she hit send, she was terrified.

But her terror was unjustified. Not only did Tom reply, he said, "Thank you for your email. Its timing is perfect and I have been having similar conversations with the Nike team here. How are you set to meet . . . at three p.m. tomorrow?" Of course, Manal agreed. And just two months later, in January 2015, Manal became the first hijabi woman featured in a Nike ad campaign. In March 2015, Nike invited Manal to become the first coach of an all-women's running club in Dubai. And finally, in March 2017, Manal was invited to Nike headquarters in Dubai for a big surprise—the company announcing Nike Pro Hijab—a line of athletic wear for hijabi women that would launch in early 2018. When she heard the news, Manal says she broke down in tears for every struggle that she'd read about on Surviving Hijab. "It was magical," she told me. "It was the first time that a multinational brand said they would cater to this segment of Muslim women. That swoosh gives us power."

Nike highlights on its website how Manal and other Muslim female athletes tested prototypes of the product for features like fit and breathability and also gave important cultural feedback, like the fact that it had to be completely opaque. And though Nike was not the first company to make a hijab for Muslim women athletes, having such a big brand behind her gave Manal an enormous sense of accomplishment. She felt that she and others in Nike Pro Hijab gear could be role models for young girls, who would now see that it's possible to both support your faith and achieve all that you want to do in the world. Manal learned that shared purpose can help a community overcome stereotypes and drive change.

• • •

NEIL GRIMMER STILL describes himself as a misfit and a punk rocker. Though he has held senior positions at IDEO and Clif Bar, his early life as an artist and as a musician in a punk band plays a huge role in informing who he is today. And when Neil became a dad, it was the misfit in him—the questioner of authority—who rebelled against the options available to parents to feed their children. There were no organic baby foods on the market, so Neil and his wife, Tana Johnson, cooked their own baby food. As two working parents with a toddler and a newborn, they were knee-deep in caring for their kids, often staying up late at night to cook baby food and pack healthy lunches for their older daughter in daycare. After ten o'clock one night, while they were pureeing the "vegetable du jour," Neil thought, "There has to be a better way. There must be a way for working parents to feed their kids healthy food, without having that trade-off between convenience and health." He committed to find a solution that could fit into busy parents' lives. With that inspiration, Neil used his creative and entrepreneurial spirit to create Plum Organics—a company built to help parents raise healthy kids with healthy food.

That purpose informed every aspect of the company—from product creation to team building and hiring to how they ran their weekly meetings—and helped them get through even difficult times. It wasn't always easy; Neil told me how he and his cofounder, Sheryl O'Loughlin, sometimes felt as if they were on an island surrounded by sharks. They had never started a company and were learning on the job. It felt as though there were many hazards, from which investors to work with to how to run manufacturing, and later to personal health issues that can arise from the stress of running a startup. They weren't sure whom they could trust. At the same time, the company's clear purpose to help families be healthier allowed them to build a close, intimate connection with everyone who worked at the company, the people on their island. Their faith and hard work paid off. Millions of parents bought Plum's food, catapulting Plum Organics to become the number one organic baby food company in the United States.

Plum sales grew to $80 million in six years and received enormous interest from strategic partners and private equity firms. After a key meeting with Campbell Soup CEO Denise Morrison, with whom Neil felt a strong connection, he and his board decided to sell Plum Organics to Campbell Soup in 2013. Campbell's delivered on its promises both to invest resources in Plum and to stay true to its mission: that same year, Campbell's allowed Plum to continue its conversion to a public benefit corporation (PBC), a type of legal incorporation for social enterprises that compels them to serve stakeholders as well as shareholders. At the time, Plum was the only wholly-owned subsidiary of a public company to legally become a PBC. Not only has Plum Organics continued to grow, but it also was at the forefront of an enormous trend driving gains in the organic baby food category. Due to the growing concern parents have about the safety of the foods their children eat, the organic prepared baby food segment is expected to account for nearly 76 percent of the total baby food market by 2020. As Neil saw, a sense of shared purpose can be incredibly powerful fuel to help a new idea catch fire.

• • •

MEGAN GRASSELL WASN'T even a senior in high school in 2014 when she founded Yellowberry, a company that makes age-appropriate bras for tween and teen girls. On a frustrating shopping trip to look for a first bra for her thirteen-year-old sister, they spent hours going to different stores but couldn't find a single bra that wasn't highly sexualized, padded, or push-up. That's when Megan decided to make her own—even though she had no idea how to start a business or create an undergarment from scratch. She told me, "I had this epiphany: Why couldn't I make this product and create a brand to make this an empowering time that every girl goes through in her life?"

She became obsessed with the idea and jumped in right away, even though she wasn't familiar with all the details. Some things went well from the start and others didn't. She thought, "Okay, to make a bra, I guess you need fabric," so she shopped for material on the Internet, choosing fabrics by color and not realizing that she had chosen sailboat canvas material, which didn't make a great first prototype. She was ultimately able to find a seamstress to work with her to create several different prototypes and used the bulk of her savings to hire a manufacturer to make the first four hundred bras, which was all she could afford.

After creating that first set of bras, Megan realized she needed more funds to help get the company off the ground. So she did what thousands of cash-strapped entrepreneurs do: she launched a Kickstarter campaign. It got off to a slow start. For the first few months, she raised only about $200—especially embarrassing because her friends and classmates could track her Kickstarter online and see that she had raised less than 1 percent of her $25,000 goal. Instead of giving up, Megan started looking online for companies or people who might support her product. She sent cold e-mails explaining her mission and her story to about two hundred people, and although just one of them responded, it worked. A company called A Mighty Girl posted about Yellowberry on its website and Facebook page after receiving Megan's message. Less than twenty-four hours later, her Kickstarter campaign had raised $25,000. Getting these early influencers on board as supporters of her movement was critical to its success.

Ultimately, Megan raised over $40,000 in her Kickstarter campaign, and her first line of products—with style names like Bug Bite, Tiny Teton, and Tweetheart—sold out quickly. Her commitment goes beyond just business success; she put her college career on hold and even gave up dreams of competing in the Olympics (she was a nationally ranked competitive ski racer) to continue to fight against the sexualization of young girls. She had a clear sense of her vision from the beginning, wanting to be a brand that could develop alongside girls, supporting and inspiring them and letting them know it's okay to grow up at their own pace.

She called the company Yellowberry as a nod to how important it is to give girls time to develop—to have "yellow" stages before becoming a red berry. The vision for Megan's movement is to "support girls through each stage of their journey to become confident and extraordinary young women." And her movement is growing, as large retailers like Nordstrom carried Yellowberry bras, popular brands like Aerie partnered with Megan to spread Yellowberry's message, and sales grew all over the world. As Yellowberry expanded, Megan was widely applauded: she was featured in the 2014 lists for *Time* magazine's 25 Most Influential Teens and the *Huffington Post's* 14 Most Fearless Teens, and the 2016 list of *Forbes's* 30 Under 30.

Megan's customers love Yellowberry, and you can see their deep appreciation in messages they post to the company on Facebook, with comments like, "FANTASTIC bras for my girls. Just got our first order and we are thrilled. I'm thinking about hosting a trunk show to pass this wonderful product along to my friends," and pictures of girls enjoying wearing their Yellowberries (all taken from the back, which is the company's mission-aligned approach to taking photos of young girls in their bras, "standing behind them to support them as they take on the world"). This appreciation from her customers reaffirms her purpose and propels Megan; as she described in a *Forbes* interview in 2017, "One of my absolute favorite things is that we have a lot of people in our community who write incredibly heartfelt messages to us about their experience with Yellowberry and how their daughter feels now that she wears Yellowberry products. To this day, it's a really easy way for me to get teary. I respond personally to each and every one that I can, and I am forever grateful for not only their business but for their support in our mission." Megan realized that tapping into a community's shared purpose could help make her dream a reality.

THE LEADERSHIP THREAD

WHY IS IT that Manal, Neil, and Megan succeeded when many other entrepreneurs and activists with equally noble goals failed? Is it because they were effective leaders with good ideas that came at the right time? Perhaps. But if you look closer, they all have one thing in common—what they did was start movements.

Movements happen when many people unite around a common purpose. Manal, Neil, and Megan each mobilized people around a purpose they were passionate about—whether it was to change stereotypes about hijabi women, make healthy food available to babies, or fight the sexualization of teenagers. They built their movements by empowering people around them both to *serve* the purpose and to *spread* the movement even further.

Why are movements so powerful? Purpose is contagious. Movements grow and spread with a force of their own to create communities of people, each burning to make the change happen. While movements are often sparked by the actions and conviction of an effective leader, they succeed when those movement starters build up other leaders within the community and everyone plays a role in driving change.

It may sound simple to do. But to get an idea of how powerful movements are, think about your daily life. Many of us lead our busy lives without stopping to think about what drives us and what's truly important to us. We manage our jobs and personal lives—and perhaps also our teams at work—skillfully, but often without connecting them to our beliefs and core values. Much has been written about the difference between managers and leaders, but most agree that managers focus more on tactics and day-to-day operations, while leaders inspire others to follow in their footsteps.

I propose a new view of leadership. As I've learned in my career spanning companies from Facebook and Google to Change.org, the most effective leaders are movement starters. Movement starters take leadership a step further. They don't just persuade people to follow them; people join and support movement starters to generate positive change. People like Manal, Neil, and Megan start with purpose and broadcast it far and wide to find support. These leaders aren't powerful because of the titles on their business cards; they are powerful because they have their mission and values front and center, and their clarity of purpose and strength of conviction inspire others to join them—to start a movement.

I've seen that this is true throughout my career, in both the business and activism worlds. In my role as the head of Groups at Facebook, I support millions of people who start communities that mobilize billions of other people around shared passions and experiences. As the former president and COO of Change.org, I witnessed regular people starting more than 1,000 petitions a day on the causes that mattered to them, and those petitions drove real change, with more than a dozen campaigns on Change.org now winning every day, achieving the change they wanted. And from my vantage point in Silicon Valley, I have spent nearly twenty years working with people whose ideas helped to build companies that make our world better. These are regular people—just like you and me—who stand up and do something about the problems they see in the world. People who are committed to ending bullying and violence against women. People who want others to have access to better education, excellent medical treatment, and cleaner water. People who want to improve the lives of people with disabilities, bring safety and equality to the LGBTQ community, and so much more.

If you've assumed that these ideas apply only to activists—just wait. One of the things that surprised me most after I joined

Change.org in 2013—and what may surprise you as well—was how similar the leadership skills were between movement starters in the social change world and those in the business world. The fact is that leadership skills don't discriminate. Successful leadership requires you to create a clear vision of what you want to achieve, inspire other people to work with you toward that vision, often persuade people in power (decision-makers) to do things you want them to do, overcome obstacles that may arise, and then just not give up until the vision is achieved. These skills are the common thread of leadership among movement starters in all sectors, all causes, and all industries. Those leaders who frame their work as movements with passionate followers will ultimately build the strongest teams and have the most success, whether working to change policies and laws, creating new brands or companies, and anything in between.

SMALL ACTIONS MATTER

ONE OF THE top social organizers in the world, Sara El-Amine, who was the executive director of President Obama's Organizing for Action and is now the director of advocacy at the Chan Zuckerberg Initiative, said at the Broadbent Institute's 2016 Progress Summit in Ottawa, "Change doesn't happen inside the halls of power. Change happens at kitchen tables, in living rooms, in training sessions like this one, but it doesn't happen in the White House, the United Nations or the halls of Parliament."

So if people are what matter—if individuals create change, not big institutions like governments or corporations—then what holds us back and keeps us from doing something, anything, to get an idea started? The biggest reason I've seen is fear that our actions don't matter, and that they won't measure up to the change instigated by huge and historically significant movements like the civil rights movement in the 1960s or the movement for marriage equality. But the truth is that what matters to the person or people who start any movement defines its scope. Just because the movements we traditionally think of are the largest ones, like the Arab Spring or Black Lives Matter, doesn't mean that changes people make in their small towns, their schools, or their workplaces aren't movements, and crucial ones at that. People are protecting local parks and monuments, they are persuading companies to recycle, they are making policies fairer at their schools, and so much more.

In fact, you should never discount the power of small actions; sometimes they are precisely the thing that prompts larger future actions, both in yourself and in others. A landmark study from 1966, "Compliance without Pressure: The Foot-in-the-Door Technique," by Jonathan Freedman and Scott Fraser of Stanford University, showed that by first asking people to do something small enough that's easy to say yes to, people were more likely to say yes to a larger request later. This technique works based on the principle that people want to appear consistent in their behaviors.

In social organizing, this technique is referred to as a "ladder of engagement"; you start by asking for a lightweight action—a signature, a "like" on a Facebook page, watching a short video, etc.—and then move people up the ladder to higher engagement actions, like sharing, donating, or volunteering. Sometimes petition signatures on Change.org, for example, are criticized as "slacktivism," or being too easy a way to get involved, but people often neglect to see that a signature may be a first step toward something bigger. And, in fact, people who take the small action of signing are then later more likely to take follow-on actions like sharing, commenting, calling or tweeting a decision-maker, donating money, or showing up in person at an event. More than 47 percent of people who sign petitions on Change.org go on to take at least one further action.

Every small action is important, and they all add up. If you look at winning campaigns on Change.org, 40 percent of them have fewer than two hundred signatures. Sometimes change doesn't require millions of people to make it happen; it just requires the right set of relevant people speaking up. And when some changes require mass mobilization, we should remind ourselves that movements that start small can grow into larger national or global ones, as we've seen with causes like the banning of plastic bags and the push for cage-free eggs.

Business ideas can become enormous movements as well. Sometimes one insight starts a revolution, as companies like Lyft, Airbnb, and TaskRabbit reimagine how work is done; entrepreneurs at companies like Google, Facebook, Amazon, Apple, and Tesla push to make the world more connected, easier to navigate, better for the environment, and massively more convenient; and PBCs that "benefit the public" like Plum Organics, Change.org, Method, and Kickstarter show that it's possible to be financially successful and to improve the world.

And while purpose-driven businesses are more effective at driving change, it turns out that they also get better results by other measures. According to John Kotter and James Heskett, authors of *Corporate Culture and Performance*, purposeful companies had consistently higher stock prices—by a factor of twelve—than non-values-driven organizations. *The Business Case for Purpose*, a report from Harvard Business Review Analytics sponsored by the EY Beacon Institute, contends that companies that "harness the power of purpose to drive performance and profitability enjoy a distinct competitive advantage"—58 percent of companies with a clearly articulated sense of purpose in their corporate mission reported growth of more than 10 percent during the three years they were followed, as compared with 42 percent of companies that don't prioritize purpose. And shared values also drive brand relationships: 64 percent of consumers say that a company's values are the main reason they choose to do business with a brand. Within companies, purpose has benefits like increased productivity, employee retention, and innovation. Reid Hoffman, executive chairman and cofounder of LinkedIn, has said, "Now, more and more professionals look for positions at companies where they can create meaningful impact and experience personal growth. Companies that understand the increasing emphasis of purpose in today's professional landscape improve their ability to attract such employees and also their ability to retain them for longer periods of time." In a wide range of organizations, I have personally seen countless times in my own experience that a sense of being part of something meaningful leads people to feel more engaged, to be more creative, and to create stronger working relationships with colleagues, all leading to better results.

Whether in business or in more traditional activism, movements start with just a few individuals and then ripple outward. We each may believe that some ideas have more or less merit than others. But the truth is, it doesn't matter. It's about what matters to you. If you are willing to step up and say, "Why *not* me? Why shouldn't I be the one to solve that problem or propose that change?" and if you can use the lessons from this book to help inspire others to join you, then you are well on your way to starting your own movement, whatever it may be.

WE ARE THE HOPE

BEYOND OUR OWN personal fulfillment, there's an even more important reason to start and lead a movement—*the world needs hope.*

We live in a world that is increasingly divided, angry, and scared, torn apart by war, political division, and rising racism and bigotry. A world where nuclear proliferation is again an increasing threat; where climate change places entire species, cities, and ultimately our planet at risk; where young girls are being denied education, trafficked, and sold into marriages; and where it seems like we are more divided in our worldviews than ever before. All of these challenges can be overwhelming.

The thing is, I believe we already have hope. It lives within all of us and appears in what we do and say, and how we treat each other. It's vibrant in some of us and more dormant in others, but at our core, the hope we so desperately need already exists within us. We *are* the leaders the world needs right now. Look past the heartbreaking headlines of violence and intolerance, and you'll find stories of profound kindness, generosity, and courage, stories like Manal's, Neil's, and Megan's.

These stories have inspired me to start my own movement—to spread the idea that we can all start movements—and I hope that they will encourage you to start your own as well. This book will walk you through the steps that successful leaders take on their path to building movements, whether they are activists or entrepreneurs, as told through the stories of real people, and sometimes surprising people, who have already done it. And some of the stories in the book are from my own experience—starting and leading a nonprofit and later a tech company, working as a tech exec at Yahoo!, Google, Change.org, and now Facebook, and also in my role as mother, sister, daughter, and wife—including my failures and triumphs along the way. This chapter covers the power of purpose and provides some examples of different kinds of movements, showing that anyone is capable of starting one. In Chapter 2, we'll talk about how movements get started and about finding the courage to step up to the plate and lead. Chapter 3 pushes you to clarify and articulate your vision and highlights techniques to get your first supporters on board. Chapter 4 covers skills and tips to effectively influence decision-makers. In Chapter 5, we'll discuss how to inspire people who join your movement and keep them motivated as part of your team. Chapter 6 talks about how to handle criticism, which often increases as your movement builds, and Chapter 7 explains how to manage obstacles and leverage failure to your advantage. This book is not a tactical primer— it won't walk you through detailed steps of how to stage a rally, or create a product road map, or even start a petition—there are plenty of other sources available to do those things. Instead, it is meant to give you the tools to become the leader of a movement, to create vision, to inspire people, to persuade those in power, to manage through seemingly insurmountable obstacles—to lead change.

We all have the power to make a difference. Maybe you'll start your own campaign and see it through to victory, overcoming obstacles and mobilizing supporters. Or maybe you'll join someone else's movement, adding your voice to a chorus that proclaims, "This matters." You might start a community of passionate people who can then mobilize to create change. Or maybe you'll propose a new idea that could make your workplace better or start a new business that solves a big problem. Whatever you do, action, creativity, and passion count. Now more than ever.

And you already have most of the tools you need. In fact, we all have the power to inspire people and spark movements around issues that matter. Whatever your movement or your cause, you have the ability to affect people's lives. This book is intended to share stories of other movement leaders—including some unlikely ones— to inspire you and practical tips to empower you so that you, too, can create hope in the world and live a purposeful life. Whereas managers accept the world as it is, movement starters burn with the passion to make it more just, equitable, and engaging. We all need to make a choice: Are we managers or movement starters?

2

SPARK A STANDING OVATION

Getting started

The doing is the thing. The talking and worrying and thinking is not the thing.

—Amy Poehler

BE THE FIRST ONE TO CLAP

WATCHING ORDINARY PEOPLE make extraordinary change happen every day in my position at Change.org inspired me to write a book about how everyone—from managers to budding entrepreneurs and from parents to teenagers to retirees—can start their own movements. I believe wholeheartedly that every single person has the capacity to start and lead a movement that changes the world; you don't need to be Nelson Mandela or Gloria Steinem to inspire change. Even the biggest movements in history were sparked by relatively small but critically important actions of key people along the way. The civil rights movement would not have been the same without Rosa Parks and the sit-in movement sparked by the Greensboro Four. Historian David Carter's research showed that it was homeless youth who first resisted police in the Stonewall riots that ultimately led to the gay rights movement. And the Americans with Disabilities Act of 1990 was successful thanks to the stories of individuals such as a woman with cerebral palsy who was denied access to a movie theater, and a wheelchair-bound Vietnam veteran who could not get on and off the bus and faced employment discrimination.

Tiffany Shlain, a filmmaker and founder of the Webby Awards, created a great short film called *50/50*. In it, she talks about the number of women who have been elected heads of state and why that number is still so small—only fifty. Shlain interviews Laura Liswood, the secretary general of the UN Foundation Council of Women World Leaders, which works with all the women who currently lead countries across the globe. Liswood sees firsthand what leads to major change—in her case, to the election of female leaders—and she, too, sees change as something that starts with a small action that grows much bigger. She says, "Change itself goes from the unthinkable, to the impossible, to the inevitable, but someone has to move it along. I often liken it to a standing ovation. A few people jump up and say this is the best thing that they have ever seen, and another larger group gets up and says yes, yes this was just excellent, and then a large group gets up and says yeah, yeah, this was okay, and finally the last group gets up because they can't see the stage." Similarly with movements, if you know your goal and focus on your first step as a starting point—what starts small can become enormous.

As the mother of two daughters who dance, I get to witness this type of "ripple effect" in action at their performances all the time.

When a particular dancer does a long set of especially good turns or a difficult acrobatic trick, often a single member of the audience will start clapping, and it's a nearly instantaneous ripple, with other people quickly joining in to clap, too. (Okay, I admit that my kids are usually highly embarrassed by this because the first person clapping is often me . . .) You start a movement when you're the first one to stand up and clap.

ONE PERSON CAN START A CHAIN REACTION

THAT FIRST CLAP can be very small. On June 17, 2013, thirty-four-year-old Erdem Gündüz walked to the middle of Istanbul's busy Taksim Square and stood completely still. He stood still there with his hands in his pockets for eight hours, from 6:00 p.m. until 2:00 a.m., in peaceful silent protest after the removal of a tent city created there by activists and demonstrators who had been brutalized by police.

Although for the first several hours he stood alone, after a few hours several people joined him, then more and more until hundreds of people were standing there together with him. "Standing Man," as Gündüz was soon called, inspired people not only in Taksim Square but also across the country, and then around the world. His actions went viral with the hashtag #duranadam (standing man). People stood in places where others had been killed by police. They stood in front of media organizations that they thought were downplaying the protests and concerns of citizens. They stood in courthouses where lawyers had been beaten and arrested for representing protesters.

His silent, motionless protest soon inspired activists around the world to strike the same pose, and sparked a feeling of international solidarity as photos and videos of the remarkable event made their way around the world via social media. By seemingly "doing nothing," Gündüz became a spark that spread worldwide, increasing awareness of the issues that citizens are facing in Turkey. And though the challenges there continue, this silent movement brought attention to the situation at a critical time and was an important moment in a continuing march.

Erdem Gündüz standing in Taksim Square   MARCO LONGARI/STAFF

If that sounds too remote an example, consider this. When I first got to college, I was a young and bright-eyed coxswain on the rowing team. The coxswain, or "cox," sits in the back of the boat on a rowing team and is responsible for the steering and speed of the boat and improving the team's technique during practice. The cox also creates strategy and motivates and coaches the crew during races.

I coxed the men's crew team for two years in high school at Pacific Rowing Club in San Francisco, which was an incredible experience for me, helping me build not only my leadership skills but also my self-confidence at an age when confidence doesn't always come easily for teenage girls. I knew I wanted to continue coxing and assumed I would cox the men's team in college as well. But when I got to Cornell and told them I wanted to cox the men, they said no, that it wasn't possible for a woman to cox the men's crew: only men could be on the men's team and only women could be on the women's team.

Their response made no sense to me.

Because, really, why not?

When I asked them that, this was the answer: "Well, the team is all men, and you might be distracting to them." Clearly, that was an inadequate answer, though one that unfortunately endures. Women scientists who were told they might be too distracting to the male scientists in their labs sent a flood of #distractinglysexy tweets in 2015. (My favorite was from @SarahMDurant—"Nothing like a sample tube full of cheetah poop to make you #distractinglysexy.")

All the coaches' answers felt like excuses, so I asked them, "Why don't you just let me try out? If I turn out to be bad at it, then don't take me on the team. But I have experience and believe I'm actually quite good at it, so let me at least give it a shot."

Sorry, they said. *It's policy.*

Adding to my frustration from not understanding "policy" as the reason was that the qualifications for the role don't have anything to do with gender. In fact, they might slightly favor women. Good coxswains are strategic, calm under pressure, good multitaskers, and are excellent at understanding and motivating their teams. Research has shown that women are actually better at several of the key skills a great coxswain needs, including cognitive empathy, multitasking, and even performing under pressure, at least as measured in some sports. *And* coxswains need to be small and light. (The target weight for collegiate coxswains is 120 pounds for men's and 110 pounds for women's.) So yes, not only are women generally quite good at the skills required, but they are also often closer to the target weight than men.

I knew that I was qualified and believed I would be an asset to the men's crew team, so I kept trying. I went to two or three different coaches on the men's team, and they all gave me the same answer—a flat-out no. I went to the athletic director of the university and told him that I didn't think their policy made any sense, and he, too, said no. Like the other coaches, he didn't understand why I cared so much, why it mattered. Why wouldn't I just cox for the women? I didn't want my previous experience to go to waste, and I wholeheartedly believed I would be excellent at coxing men. And while I was fighting this particular battle for myself, I didn't believe any woman should have to settle for a no because of her gender.

But in the end, though I was passionate about this cause and willing to fight for it, I gave in. After going up through the ranks of decision-makers at the university, I felt that I'd taken it as far as I could. I just didn't know what else to do. Looking back, I am a bit disappointed in myself that I let go of the fight so easily. I wonder, if the Internet had existed then (am I really that old?), whether I might have tried using social media or starting an online petition or doing something else to call attention to an issue that I believed needed reconsideration. Hindsight is twenty-twenty, so I'll really never know. At the time, though, I let it go and joined the women's team as coxswain.

However, it turns out that even without social media or a petition, those small actions I took *did* matter. About three months into the semester, I got a call from the athletic director. "We've been talking about it ever since you came to us, and we've changed our minds. We're going to change the policy. So if you'd like, you can cox the men's team." After discussing it more, they decided it made sense to base the role on skill (and size) rather than on gender.

I was surprised by their reversal and that they were actually going to change their policy—one that had been discriminatory. While I didn't switch to the men's team out of my already deep-seated loyalty to the women's team, I was heartened to know that I had encouraged them to change the policy. And I felt even better when my freshman Big Red boat of amazing women rowers I coxed won the national championship that year for our division.

The most fulfilling part of the athletic department's change in policy wasn't the outcome for me. It was knowing that, because of this decision, other women would not have to fight the same battle. Helping to change that one policy in college gave me my first taste of what it felt like to stand up for something I believed in. After this experience, I realized that even small actions, and one lone voice, could make a lasting difference. A few years ago, when I was back at Cornell speaking with the crew team, I asked one of the rowers how many of the coxswains on the men's team were women. "Almost all of them," she said. "It just makes sense, right?"

It does make sense, and not just because there's a size requirement for the job, which happens to be easier for women to fill than men. Women coxing men's crew has now become the norm at most universities, because they're *good at it.*

• • •

YOU CAN SEE how consequential one small action can be. Now imagine what a difference the accumulation of many small actions can make. The combined power of many small actions, and many individuals taking action, is the only thing that truly has the power to create change.

WHAT HOLDS US BACK

ALL THAT SAID, it can be difficult to get started—to get up in front of everyone to stand up and clap. Sara El-Amine, the social change veteran whom I introduced in the last chapter, told me that there are four basic reasons why most people don't take action to try to create change:

- They don't believe they can succeed.
- They lack support.
- They don't have the tools.
- They have no funding.

While all of these obstacles need to be overcome in order to create forward momentum for a cause you want to support or an idea you want to pursue and bring to fruition, it's that first one—not believing in your own ability to effect change—that keeps most people from getting started. It is why it's so important to hear the stories of people who have taken action and successfully made change happen in order to imagine yourself actually doing the thing you dream of doing. The more you see examples of ordinary people doing extraordinary things for causes they believe in, the more you'll start believing that you, too, can make a difference. That anyone can do this.

Because anyone *can* do this.

So how do we transform our good intentions into taking steps to create change? How do we ignore the voice that says "I can't" or "Why bother?" and instead see that hope and a sense of purpose are all we really need to make a difference?

•   •   •

SOMETIMES WHAT KEEPS us from stepping forward to take action is a misplaced sense that we haven't earned the right to have a voice in certain movements, that perhaps we don't belong in particular fights in our communities or in our companies because we are outsiders to those struggles. I know I've felt this way many times. As I write about my life, it's impossible for me not to acknowledge how much privilege I've had as a white American born to upper-middle-class parents. I also had what Ben Rattray, the founder of Change.org, calls "love privilege" because I always felt loved and supported by my family. All of these advantages have certainly made my life easier, and for that I'm grateful.

And as a woman and a Jew, I've gotten a glimpse into what it feels like to know that the world may treat you differently just because of who you are. I have also seen some of the experiences of my sister Bonnie, who is black and joined our family in her teens, which gives me a small window into the challenges she encounters. Not only have I observed the direct racism she faces, but in talking with her to try to understand more about her experience, I have also learned from her about the often indirect racism she sees. Examples such as people saying to her, "Oh, you're not black," because she grew up in a white neighborhood and went to mainly white private schools, a comment people may mean as a compliment, but which in itself is deeply hurtful and ignores the reality of her daily experience of being black in America.

This is complicated stuff. Though people don't often talk about race and privilege, we should. Only by being open to hearing and understanding each other's stories can we break down walls of misunderstanding and hate over time. We shouldn't let fear of saying the wrong thing stop us from taking action or even just asking questions, especially if we have good intentions. We may make mistakes in how we go about trying to be an ally, but it's better than not trying at all. And by engaging in the conversation and participating in the movements of groups we ourselves are not a part of, we can learn about both what makes us each unique and the bonds that tie us all together.

ASK "WHY *NOT* ME?"

THOUGH SOME OF us may come from more privilege than others, all of us have the ability to make a difference. People who come from struggle have powerful stories to tell. And people whose lives have been easier also have stories to tell. They don't need to harbor the guilt that can come with privilege, but rather take advantage of the opportunity to use that privilege to do something that matters.

My mother was the one to teach me that lesson (and many others). When my mom was still in her twenties, newly married to my dad, she received some unexpected and very difficult news: she had cancer in her parotid gland on the right side of her neck, and to treat it she would have to go through major surgery and months of radiation. It's hard to imagine how frightening that must have been for both of them as a young couple just starting out, not knowing whether she would make it through the surgery, and if she did, whether or not they would be able to have a family. Thankfully, the operation to remove the tumor was successful in saving her life. But during the procedure, the surgeon accidentally severed one of her facial nerves. Half of her face would forever be paralyzed.

I never knew my mother to look any other way. I never knew her with a different face—one that didn't cause people to stare, or ask what was wrong with her, or whisper about it without ever asking. Yet through all of this, she always handled herself with incredible grace and confidence, never complaining, never shying away from challenges, and never letting a physical setback get in her way. She put a strong, warm, half-crooked smile on life, proving to me, through her actions and behavior, that anything was possible because she believed that anything *was* possible. I watched as she changed careers in her thirties, leaving a job in speech pathology to attend business school at night. Despite the difficulty of trying to start a new career as a woman and a latecomer, and with the added stress of a physical difference she couldn't hide, my mom didn't give up. She didn't give up when night school made it difficult to meet all her other commitments, and she didn't give up when she had fifty (yes, fifty) interviews, without receiving a job offer. It was her fifty-first interview that got her foot in the door at Towers Perrin, a leading HR consulting firm where she spent the next twenty years, eventually becoming one of their most successful consulting partners.

Now that's grit.

When I look at my mother, I see someone who never once asked "Why me?" when it came to her facial paralysis or any other obstacle she's faced, but rather someone who had always said, "Why *not* me?" when it came to issues in the world she believed needed to be addressed.

Both of my parents grew up in modest surroundings, with just enough to get by, appreciative of the opportunities with which they were presented. My mom tells us stories about working her way through college and keeping a ledger of everything she spent, down to the penny, to make sure she could make it through the month. These types of experiences led my parents to a lifetime of hard work, and then later, when they became successful, to have a passion for giving back. Just as my mom never doubted her ability to improve her own life, she also never wavered in her belief that she could have a positive impact on others' lives. From donating money to causes they cared about to volunteering for the Red Cross emergency team (with supplies always in the trunk of their car) to opening our home to Bonnie, an amazing young woman in her teens who is now my third sister, my mom and dad always stepped up. They saw something that needed to be done and they did it; they saw people who were in need of help and they offered it. They always said, "Why *not* me?"

That question—Why *not* me?—is central to whether or not we will go through life daring to participate in improving the world. Will we be brave enough to take steps to make change, or will we stand back and wait for others to act?

So many of us see the injustices happening around us and feel overwhelmed or powerless to do anything. And so many of us have exciting new ideas that we believe can solve problems, but feel we don't know enough to make our dreams a reality. I have been in that position many times myself. I can look back with regret at the times I wish I had done more, been a better ally to someone in pain, fought more for the causes or ideas I believe in.

"Why *not* me?" is the voice of change and hope, the voice that allows you to take a first step toward following a purpose and creating a movement, righting wrongs and fixing what's broken in the world, or creating solutions to meet people's needs. It's what makes you stand up for what you believe in, even if your legs are shaking when you do.

PURPOSE IS AN EQUALIZER

THOUGH IT'S COMMON to be afraid that we don't have the experience or expertise to contribute to a cause, sometimes messages with meaningful purpose are the most powerful when they come from unexpected voices. Sarah Kavanagh, a socially minded teenager from Hattiesburg, Mississippi, became vegan at age twelve based on her love of animals. Because Sarah was vegan, she was conscious about ingredients in her food and drinks. So in 2012, at age fifteen, Sarah Googled the ingredients on the label of a bottle of Gatorade, her favorite sports drink, and saw an ingredient listed that she'd never heard of—brominated vegetable oil (BVO). After a bit more research, she learned that BVO, which is used to keep citrus drinks from separating and contains the same ingredient (bromine) as brominated flame retardants, was removed from the FDA's GRAS (Generally Regarded as Safe) list in 1970. Although BVO is banned in over one hundred countries, including Japan, India, and most of Europe, BVO was still in most American energy drinks and many other soft drinks. This didn't make sense to her. "I looked it up and the first article that came up was from *Scientific American* that talked about all of these crazy side effects that could be caused by BVO," she told me. "They included reduced fertility, early onset puberty, impaired neurological development—absolutely horrendous things that are caused by an ingredient in something that's supposed to be a health product and that's aimed at athletes. We knew that this was harming people. Why, if this information was so easily available, wasn't anyone talking about it? Why wasn't it something that people cared about?"

Sarah decided to take action. She was familiar with Change.org because of her support for animal rights and had signed other successful petitions, so she started one herself, asking Pepsi to remove BVO from Gatorade. She wasn't sure the company would listen. As she told me, "I did think it could work because I had seen other people do it, but it's different when you're doing it yourself. Going through a process like this, you tend to see other people on a different level than you see yourself." As a teenager, she didn't feel as if she had the authority to speak up for a cause that would require a change from a multinational corporation. Sarah voiced a fear that many of us feel: "I didn't necessarily expect anyone to care and I definitely did not expect a corporation to actually listen to us."

But Sarah's voice was powerful, and listen to her they did. In fact, it may have been because she was such an unexpected voice speaking up on this issue that she was able to get so much attention. People were signing the petition both because they cared about their health and because Sarah inspired them. And when they signed, they shared their support with their networks, which accelerated its growth dramatically. About a month after she started the campaign, it had gathered 17,000 signatures. And Sarah was really excited, thinking to herself, "Wow, these are actual people; 17,000 people have read something that I wrote, have paid attention to a cause I care about and they're standing up with me. It was really cool." Thanks to the early success, Change.org was starting to get media inquiries about Sarah's petition. Change.org staff reached out to her to let her know she had been invited to the *Today* show and *The Dr. Oz Show* as well as many other outlets to talk about her campaign and the dangers of BVO.

At *The Dr. Oz Show*, Sarah was in the greenroom with an expert from the Center for Science in the Public Interest, a prominent consumer advocacy group that focuses on food safety and nutrition and that was central to changes like the labeling and reduction of trans fats in our food. He told Sarah that he'd been trying to get BVO banned for years without much success. "He said," as Sarah recounted to me, "'I just want to let you know that our organization has been fighting for decades to do what you've done in only months.'" Incredibly, a fifteen-year-old with an online petition was able to achieve massive momentum and attract national attention in six short months, whereas more experienced advocates had been working for years to publicize their cause.

Sarah was a Gatorade fan—she wasn't doing this to hurt Pepsi as a company, she was speaking up to ask them to make the change so that she and others like her could feel confident they were being safe when continuing to drink Gatorade. And because she had created a movement of people supporting the cause, she didn't feel alone: "People would send me e-mails and would message me on

Facebook and would tweet at me. I had constant support always coming in from people, so I never felt like it was me versus a big corporation. I felt like it was me and all these people from all over the world telling Pepsi that we'd like them to change."

Though Pepsi wasn't very responsive at first, not replying to e-mails and agreeing to only a brief conversation, in January of 2013, less than three months after she started the petition, Pepsi announced it would remove BVO from Gatorade, making Sarah's campaign a success. And she didn't stop there. Her first step led to another, and then another: after she won her first campaign to have BVO removed from Gatorade, she started a campaign asking Coca-Cola to take the same ingredient out of Powerade. Ultimately, both Pepsi and Coca-Cola decided to take BVO out of *every single one of their drinks*, around the world.

Despite all of her successes, this huge turning point shocked and amazed Sarah. "When I first found out that BVO would be removed, I cried," she told me. Even talking about that moment years later made her emotional, and not just because it was a major success for a cause that she had championed. Being able to convince two enormous corporations drove home just how much power she had as an advocate. Sarah explains, "As a woman and as someone from Mississippi, from the South, I've always felt like I've had to work harder for things, which sucks, but in that moment I realized I had actually done something substantial. Something that actually mattered. It didn't matter that the odds were against me. I worked hard for this and I put all my emotions and energy into trying to change things. And it had finally happened. It was the most empowering moment of my life."

Sarah learned that even though she wasn't the most "obvious" person to start this movement, she could do it anyway, and her conviction in her purpose carried her through. "You've just got to go for it," she told me. "You can't underestimate yourself, otherwise change is never going to be made. You can't sit back and assume that somebody on a different level than you is going to do something. What's the point in being silent?"

And that's true for all our voices. Even if it feels like others might have more experience or more reason to speak up, what matters is actually doing it. If a teenager from Mississippi could start a movement to make soft drinks healthier for all of us, then you can start a movement to serve a cause you care about, too. What's important to remember is that Sarah didn't start out saying, "I'm going to get the

Sarah Kavanaugh with Dr. Oz   CHANGE.ORG

biggest soft drink companies in the world to take this ingredient out of every product they have." She started out by making a single suggestion, expressing her belief that the ingredient was unnecessary, then seeing if others would agree with her. From a fifteen-year-old's small initial action came a groundswell of support, which led to change.

IICDTICDA

FEAR STOPS MANY of us from taking action. A voice inside our head asks, *What if I fail? What if people criticize me? What if my idea is just not good?* Well, what if, instead of succumbing to that fear, we could keep moving forward despite it? One way to do that is to get practice first, by doing other things that frighten us.

When I was growing up, my family used acronyms to communicate in shorthand. It was our secret language. This was before texting, of course, so we actually had a list of translations stuck to the refrigerator to keep us fluent. There was "SYU" (Since You're Up), used when you were sitting on the couch and feeling too lazy to get something for yourself, and "FHB" (Family Hold Back), emergency code for when we would invite people over and suddenly realize that there wasn't quite enough food for everyone unless we all took a little less than usual. When I went off to college, the tradition continued with acronyms like "IMS," which stood for In My Sweats, an easy one-liner to decline evening invitations to go out with friends when you were already settled in for the night, and "GU,"

Geographically Undesirable, which described people who lived too far away to make a potential relationship practical or appealing.

You'd think with so much practice coming up with snappy acronyms that I could have done better than the horribly long IICDTICDA. But even though the clumsy pronunciation of the acronym ("icked-tickda") is inelegant, it drives many of my decisions and has helped me become the person I want to be:

If I can do this, I can do anything.

I'm not—and never have been—a fearless person, but I figured out long ago that the way for me to become less scared of doing big or unknown things was to do other things that scared me, early and often. It helped me get used to the idea of fear, and of failure, and it made other things seem easier in comparison.

The first time I put IICDTICDA to use was when my parents sent me, at fifteen, to a summer camp for troubled teens in New Mexico designed to build inner strength and grit. My parents had sent my younger sister, Deb, there the summer before, and though she had left home as a somewhat insecure and anxious tween, she came back with life-changing confidence and resilience. So the following summer they sent us both.

Of all the many activities, the one I remember most is a daylong ropes course that ended on top of a cliff where an almost completely vertical zip line awaited. I can still see myself standing there, paralyzed in fear, letting everyone go ahead of me, which only prolonged my misery. I watched each of my peers leap off the edge of the cliff and free-fall for what seemed like an eternity, until it was my turn. My friends chanted, "Ice cream and soda, pretzels and beer, come on, Jen, get your butt down here!" which, not surprisingly, I didn't find encouraging. I could have turned around and said, "I can't do this"; I was just a kid and this was just camp, after all. But somehow, even then, quitting didn't seem like an option. Instead, I thought: *Can I convince myself that if I can do this, I'll be able to do lots of other things I'm afraid of?* (Yes, even as a teenager standing on the edge of a cliff, I managed a somewhat rational thought.)

So I took that leap—literally and figuratively. And even though I hated every second of the terrifying descent of that zip line, I realized what had given me the courage to do it: as afraid as I was of jumping off that cliff, I was much more afraid of being the kind of person who would walk away from an opportunity just because I was scared.

IICDTICDA guided me to do other things that scared me, like join the volunteer fire department and spend a semester of college in the Brazilian Amazon studying rainforest ecology. Although I was originally planning to study in Italy, I wanted to make the most of the opportunity to study abroad and to push myself as far as possible outside my comfort zone. So I found the catalog from the School for International Training, and I decided on a semester in the rainforest. Unsure of what lay ahead, I packed up my belongings and hopped on a plane to the Amazon (actually, two planes, a bus, and a boat).

I knew that going to Brazil would be difficult for all the obvious reasons—the rural parts of the country where I would spend half my time were remote, without electricity or running water, and in this case also full of wild animals. And yet, as it turned out, those things were not what was most challenging for me. Sure, there were some terrifying moments involving snakes, tarantulas, and giant poisonous ants. But unexpectedly, the hardest part for me was not knowing the language and being unable to communicate with the people around me. Although I had studied other Romance languages, I hadn't studied Portuguese beforehand. I knew it would be difficult, but I hadn't *truly* understood what it would feel like to think so hard; from the time I woke up to the time I went to sleep, I had a headache every day and felt as helpless as a child. In this case, hard work paid off; by the end of my time in Brazil, I was a strong communicator (though no guarantees on the accuracy of my Portuguese grammar). But experiencing the frustration of not being able to communicate as easily as I was used to gave me an enormous amount of empathy for people who face language and cultural barriers, which sticks with me to this day. Overall, the experience gave me confidence in my ability to thrive in many other new situations. It's much easier to tackle difficult challenges in your life and career if you push yourself early to try things you haven't done before. And the scarier the better—within reason, of course.

Note that putting yourself in frightening situations to practice overcoming fear doesn't mean that you won't still feel afraid. Like the time I went to India to visit one of our Change.org teams (with my family in tow) and agreed to go on the collectively-decided-upon group activity: a cycling tour of Old Delhi.

Now, I realize that thousands of people who live in Delhi ride bicycles through this part of the city every day, so it is not in and of itself a challenging activity, but anyone who knows me well knows that I'm the least likely person to want to cycle through one of the most congested cities in the world. I grew up in San Francisco, where the steep hills make bike riding seem more like an extreme sport. Consequently, I didn't learn to ride a bicycle until my twenties (which, by the way, is quite embarrassing because I still fell a lot when I was learning, and most people do not expect to see adults falling off their bikes).

In the abstract, the challenge made me nervous enough. But once I was actually on my bike, with my helmet on and my husband and two daughters in front of me, and speeding motorcycles, tuk tuks, other cyclists, pedestrians, and several dozen cows swarming all around me, my nervousness escalated to a full state of panic. I was terrified for myself as well as for my family—especially my young daughters. I'm sure my team would have understood and let me off the hook. There would be plenty of other opportunities for good old-fashioned team building when we weren't all risking death on two wheels. But as usual, I couldn't ignore the leading-by-example voice in my head. Plus, I didn't want my daughters to be thrown off by my fear.

Aside from my hitting two people with my bicycle (luckily they weren't hurt since I was going so painfully slowly) and getting smacked in the face with a cow's tail, our Old Delhi adventure turned out to be an amazing experience. Not only did I live to tell this story, but my daughters, Rachel and Emma, who were riding in front of me the whole time, also did incredibly well. Compared to me, they were much better at navigating the traffic and all the obstacles we faced, so much so that at some point during that extremely stressful ride I had a life-epiphany moment: They were able to stare down their own fear and keep going. They were going to be okay.

I often hear entrepreneurs say that fearlessness led to their success. My successes have not been due to a lack of fear on my part but rather a result of the willingness to keep going despite my fear. I see true courage in having fear and moving forward anyway. The fight-or-flight response is so deeply woven into our DNA that risk aversion is a completely natural instinct. It's normal to be afraid of dangerous things; it's fear that keeps us from running toward truly life-threatening situations and protects us from harm. In our modern lives, though, we primarily fear failure. Many of us spend a great deal of time and energy avoiding what scares us—whether it's being adventurous in the outdoors, public speaking, asking out someone we like, or taking a chance on a new job that feels like a big risk. What if, instead of beating ourselves up for wanting to avoid risk and uncertainty and all the things that scare us, we took those chances anyway?

There is a dirty little secret that few people talk about—*the first time you do anything, you've never done it before*. It's true for everyone. It's certainly true of every single milestone in my life: the first step I took, my first day of school, my first kiss, having my first child, my first job, my first day as a manager, my first day as a CEO . . . you get the idea. And it's true for everyone else around us, no matter how impressive they may appear; they had a "first day," too. Somehow, we all manage not only to get through these firsts but also to become quite adept at those activities over time. Yet once we gain expertise, we often forget the first-day feeling and again fear failure. If, instead, we could remember the feeling of trying something new and learning we could be good at it, then when we are faced with those moments where we have an idea we want to pursue or a change we want to make, we can remind ourselves that we can do it, even if—especially if—it's difficult.

START ANYWHERE—JUST START

WITH ALL OF that in mind, remember: getting started is the most important thing you can do. Even actions that may feel inconsequential to you initially may result in a major movement. That's what happened for Alli Webb, a professional stylist who, with her brother, my longtime friend Michael Landau, cofounded Drybar, a national chain of salons devoted to blow-drying hair.

Alli had spent most of her childhood, as well as her personal and professional life, trying to tame her unruly hair until she finally mastered the art of the blowout. And she found surprising power in the simple pleasure of having her hair blow-dried. She told me, "I have naturally curly hair, and as a young girl I used to beg my mom to blow-dry my hair straight. Of course, back then I couldn't articulate it, but when my mom would blow out my hair I was so happy, and I felt so good."

Alli knew that having "challenging" hair wasn't something completely unique to her—as someone with naturally very curly hair, I can relate. So she had a hunch that other women would love getting blowouts, too. (Michael didn't get it at first. He told me, "I honestly didn't understand why a woman would need someone else to blow-dry her hair. I'm bald, and I don't dry my hair.")

Her husband, Cam, who did advertising, design, and branding, made her a website. "We called it Straight at Home," she told me. "Cam said that if we had a great website, people would call me, and they did. I posted the site on lots of mommy blogs, and off I went." Alli underscored that the early incarnation of Drybar was just a way to get out of the house and earn a little extra cash doing something she enjoyed. She was charging forty dollars per blowout, had a duffel bag full of brushes and hair products, and started going to all these "mommy friends'" houses to do their hair. She was very fulfilled by what she was doing and that she was able to do it on her own schedule.

And then her business started growing. People loved it—she had the start of a movement on her hands because she was building something great. As she told me, "Then this little business started booming. It wasn't until I got really busy and had more demand than supply of me that I hit a crossroads: Do I expand and hire other stylists to fill this demand? Michael and I started talking about opening an actual brick-and-mortar shop so that these women could come to me instead of me going to them. That's how the whole thing came to be. But it was still just going to be one shop. There was never a grand plan for what has happened."

So she started small and she wasn't quite sure where it would lead. She had one other key insight along the way, which was that she didn't have to do everything on her own. In fact, both Alli and Michael credit the success of Drybar to the fact that there were four partners, each with unique skills, that together created the right blend of leadership they needed to be successful. The business started with Alli, Cam, Michael, and their friend Josh Heitler, an incredible architect who agreed to design the first store in exchange for equity in the company. As Michael told me, "We had this perfect storm of an unbelievable designer and architect who was putting his blood, sweat, and tears into the business. We had Cam, who was this crazy-talented marketing and advertising guy who we would never have been able to afford, but he's Alli's husband. And then we had Alli, who had the idea, and the hair knowledge, of how to build this whole thing. And then me with the business side of it. So it all kind of came together."

Alli had partners to help her move that idea first to a single brick-and-mortar store in Brentwood, California, and then to create what Drybar has now become—a popular, fast-growing brand with over seventy locations in the United States and Canada and a successful product line sold at Sephora, Nordstrom, and other retailers.

The Drybar movement came with a major insight behind it: *when people look good, they feel good.* And that gives them confidence to achieve other goals. So this idea that started as a very small business ended up growing rapidly, with the crucial purpose of helping women feel more confident about themselves. Michael finally came to that understanding a bit later. As he told me: "It took me longer to understand what Cam and Alli knew, but there was this personal moment where I realized that during my freshman year of college I started losing my hair, and it changed me. I was always an extrovert my whole life, but when I lost my hair I didn't feel put together. One of our clients pointed out the correlation, that she doesn't feel put together unless she comes to Drybar, so I thought, 'Oh my God, if a woman feels a fraction of what I felt in college when I was losing my hair, then I understand what a giant opportunity this is.'"

And it is a huge opportunity, both to give people the confidence that comes from feeling like they look great and to build a huge business. Their customers actively talk about what a confidence-boosting experience a visit to Drybar is, as you can see in tweets like these: "Thanks @theDrybar! Yall always make me feel so confident and have the best stylists!" from @BelindaK04 and "Love starting my day @theDrybar. I always feel more confident than when I came in with frizz. Thanks for that #drybarhouston #curlyhairprob" from @claudiahualde. The Drybar movement grows every day, and their potential customers want it to get even bigger. On the Drybar Facebook page, you can see people asking for Drybar to come to their towns all across the United States:

"Please bring Drybar to Evanston"

"Please come to Chapel Hill, NC!"

"Any chance that you have a drybar opening in Buffalo, NY in the future? (Please say yes)"

"Please come to Madison, Wisconsin!!! You're needed here!"

"When will you have a shop west of Westlake, CA!!?? You need to come to Carpinteria!! Santa Barbara!!"

Alli's initial step led to what is now a nationwide movement, even though that wasn't her expectation at the start.

We all have the power to create change, and the power to lead our own movements, whether they are small or large, local or national, a new law or a new business. They all start in the same way, with one person willing to take a risk—to be the first one to stand up and clap.

3

BREATHE LIFE INTO YOUR VISION

Transforming intention into action

Without vision, even the most focused passion is a battery without a device.

—KEN AULETTA

VISION FIRST

THE FIRST STEP to any successful movement is to create a clear and compelling vision of what that movement intends to achieve. A vision is your *desired future*; the purpose is the reason *why* you want it. Ask yourself: How do you want the world to look? Why does it matter for the world to change in this way? The most successful movements have both a clear vision and a clear purpose to help others understand where you are trying to go and why they should help.

Movements are dynamic because they're driven by a vision with a purpose. Even those people we've met previously in this book who started with one small action had a clear vision and purpose from the beginning. In Megan Grassell's world, young girls can buy age-appropriate bras because girls like her sister need better choices that let them grow up at their own pace. In Neil Grimmer's, parents can easily buy organic food for their infants because busy parents deserve to give their babies healthy food.

People often create both vision statements and mission statements when they start new organizations: a vision statement to explain the *desired future* and a mission statement to show *what the organization intends to do* in order to achieve that vision. As an example, Change.org's *mission* is "to empower people everywhere to create the change they want to see" with the goal of enacting its *vision* of "a world where no one is powerless." The hypothesis is that empowering people to create change on a large enough scale should lead to the desired future of a world where no one is powerless.

Once you have a clear vision (the desired future or the where) and purpose (the why), you can then create a mission (the what), strategies and tactics (the how), and goals and objectives (the how well) so you can make sure that you are on the right path toward achieving your vision. And when the journey gets difficult, your vision serves as a compass—both for you and your team. A movement simply cannot exist without a vision to rally people around, and the more clearly articulated that vision is, the easier it will be to mobilize people to achieve it.

Communicate your vision with visceral stories to help people deeply understand what it is and why it matters. We naturally find personal stories memorable, like Megan bra shopping with her sister, or Neil and his wife making baby food late at night; they help us see the motivations for their movements. You can also highlight individual stories to show how the vision will have an impact on people rather than leaving it in broad, general terms. Politicians are masters of this technique. While advocating for particular policies, they often invite individuals or families who might be affected to join the audience at a speech they are giving. The presence of these people makes vision and purpose more accessible.

Marshall Ganz, a senior lecturer in public policy at the Harvard Kennedy School of Government and a social organizing expert well known for his work with the United Farm Workers, goes a level deeper in utilizing storytelling as a strategy. He argues that a public narrative has three parts: a story of self, a story of us, and a story of now. A story of self covers your own personal purpose—your calling and why it matters to you. It may include personal challenges you have had to overcome or particular people or experiences that motivate you. A story of us describes the community of people you want to join you, and what you have in common that will inspire them to do so. Here you should focus on stories about shared identity and values and how those shared values can persuade them to act. And a story of now explains the urgency around acting quickly. In this story, Ganz suggests that you focus on the challenge you are facing jointly with your supporters, specific actions you want them to take, and the vision that can be achieved if they take this action with you now. Ganz has published worksheets you can find online that will walk you through how to create your own public narrative using story of self, story of us, and story of now.

Storytelling is a skill that social organizers apply excellently, and one that business leaders should consider exercising more often.

When you give your vision—an abstract goal—a clear story that shows how it affects individuals, it has exponentially more impact. I've found that being able to communicate my vision in a heartfelt and concrete way paid off at many points in my career. I often tell the story of a movement close to my heart: getting benefits for pregnant mothers in the workplace. Once leaders heard examples of real women who were trying to pump milk in bathroom stalls or who could no longer get out of their car doors in the late stages of their pregnancies when the parking spaces were too close together (yes, that happened to me), the policies at many companies changed. (Note that there is still more to do in bringing equal treatment to all women on this front.)

THE WINNING COMBINATION FOR A MOVEMENT IS:

a clearly articulated vision that paints a picture of the way you want the world to look

+

a clear purpose behind *why* that vision matters to you and others

+

one or more compelling stories that help bring your vision and purpose to life

STORIES THAT GIVE VISION MEANING

HANK HUNT HAD a picture-perfect life. He grew up in Little Rock, Arkansas; he was a "typical southern boy who got dirty and popped wheelies on bicycles and pulled girls' ponytails." He moved to Texas in 1972 and married his high school sweetheart, and they had two little girls. Hank joined the armed forces as a military police officer and says he believes he did a lot of good in that job. He didn't intend to start a movement or change the world in a big way, but he says he's "always been the kind of person that if I see somebody that needs some help, I do what I can to help them."

And then on December 1, 2013, tragedy struck. Hank's wife was in Fort Worth at a Christmas bazaar, and he was home when she called around lunchtime. She told Hank that she couldn't reach their daughter, Kari, which didn't seem that out of the ordinary. But a few minutes later when he tried several times and got no answer, he felt the first twinge of concern, since his daughter almost always answered his calls. Then his wife told him that Kari's husband had just posted, "Oh my God, I snapped," on social media. Now Hank was really worried. He called the police department and the hospital to see if Kari had been admitted or whether they had been called to a domestic disturbance. He knew something was wrong when the person at the police department said, "Can I have a detective call you back?"

And something *was* very wrong. As Hank would soon find out, his daughter, Kari, was stabbed by her estranged husband in a hotel bathroom while her three children, ages two, four, and nine, were in the bedroom on the other side of the thin wall. Amid their mother's screams, Hank's oldest grandchild had tried to dial 911 to get help for her mother, but she couldn't get the call to go through. Like most children and adults, she had no idea that in a hotel she would need to dial 9 first to get an outside line. After not being able to reach 911, she tried asking hotel employees for help and eventually reached a guest across the hall who first tried to assist, and then successfully called 911. Emergency services arrived eleven minutes after the call finally went through.

Unfortunately, it was too late. Kari died that day.

Despite his unthinkable loss, Hank has since dedicated himself tirelessly to campaigning for his vision: "Kari's Law" would require hotels and other businesses to do away with phone systems that require dialing any additional number before calling 911. Hank envisions a world where 911 would work the same way on every phone so that no other person has to face the unspeakable agony that his granddaughter did that day. As Hank described to me: "While the law may have Kari's name on it, it was my granddaughter who was the inspiration for it. When I had her in my lap at the police station after it happened, I can't even begin to describe the look on her face. It was like she was searching for something because she kept looking from eye to eye, back and forth. She said, 'Papa, I tried four times and the telephone didn't work.' And then it dawned on me: she was at a hotel, and hotel telephone systems required you to dial an extra number to get an outside line. But she didn't know that. When I saw my granddaughter's face and heard her tell me what happened, I knew it was my fault. It was everyone's fault. Every adult is to blame because we teach our children to call 911. We advertise it. It's on fire trucks, police cars, everywhere. But what's not there is: 'Call 911 unless you're in a hotel or office building or anywhere else where you have to dial an extra number to get an outside line first.' Kids would have to constantly relearn how to call 911 unless we get it changed."

When you hear Hank's story, Kari's story, and Kari's daughter's story, it's nearly impossible not to want to fix this as desperately as Hank does. Hank's story gives power to his vision to reform 911, and that vision has become a movement. More than 600,000 people signed Hank's Change.org petition, igniting a massive campaign. First, some large hotel companies, like the Marriott International Corporation, mandated that all hotels franchised under the Marriott brand update their phone system to be direct-dial 911. Then Hank was able to get Kari's Law passed in several states, including Texas, New York, Illinois, Maryland, and Tennessee. And finally the bill passed unanimously in the House of Representatives in January 2017 and in the Senate in August 2017, and President Trump signed it into law in February of 2018—an enormous victory. Hank Hunt will say he still has a ways to go in order to achieve his vision of ensuring this never happens to another child, but he's quite close now and making one hell of a difference along the way. His tragedy fuels him as well as all the other people who joined the movement for Kari's Law.

VISION GUIDES STRATEGY

HAVING A CRYSTAL clear vision also helps you adapt when things don't go the way you plan and you need to change your approach in order to realize your vision. In fact, it's fairly common that the strategies you use to achieve your vision need to evolve as the world changes and you gather more information about which strategies do and don't work. That's what happened to Chris Ategeka after gaining a deeper understanding of the problem he was trying to solve.

Chris was born in a small village in Uganda. When he was seven years old, he saw both of his parents die from AIDS within six months of each other. Despite his age, he was expected to care for his four younger siblings even as the five children became homeless and had to scrounge for food. Ultimately, they were separated to live with different families. Chris considers himself lucky. He was able to move into an orphanage and attend primary school. And later, an American family sponsored him to attend a private high school in Uganda and then helped him move to California to stay with them while he attended college. He graduated with a bachelor of science and a master's degree in mechanical engineering from U.C. Berkeley.

When Chris was nine, one of his younger brothers died while Chris and another family member were carrying him on their backs to the nearest hospital—which was ten miles away. After seeing those closest to him die without access to medical care, Chris realized the urgency of creating a world in which every human being has access to quality health care. His first entrepreneurial effort was to create a nonprofit organization, originally called Rides for Lives, to build vehicles such as motorbike ambulances to connect people in rural Ugandan communities to health and education services.

But as he learned more about the problem, he realized he would need to evolve the way he aimed to achieve his vision. His original approach assumed that getting more people to the hospital would be the key. As he explained to me: "We started off building village ambulances. When you live in a village and you have an emergency of some kind, you are pretty much out of luck. Here in America if you have an emergency, you call 911. People show up. You go to the hospital and you're saved. Over there if you have an emergency, you are pretty stuck because there's no such thing as 911."

But even though they built hundreds of vehicles and delivered thousands of patients, they kept running into the same problem. "You get someone to the hospital and there is no doctor," Chris told me. "There's no hope for one. Or if there is one, it could take two or three or four days before it's their turn to see the doctor. Sometimes people died before they got the chance to be seen."

So Chris "put his engineering hat on" and tried a second approach. Instead of bringing people to the hospital, he would bring the hospital to them. Now the doctor, the lab, and the pharmacy were all inside a single bus. And instead of the patients coming to the hospital, he brought the hospital to the patients. However, there was still a problem. When the mobile hospitals came to the villages, the lines were so long that people still couldn't get fast access to the critical health care they needed.

Seeing these extremely long lines, Chris realized that this mobile hospital approach was also unlikely to work given how few doctors were available. Whether he brought people to the hospital or brought the hospital to them, there were not enough doctors and highly trained medical workers to service the needs of the people. But Chris did not give up. He pivoted again to create Health Access Corps, whose mission is to "sustainably strengthen healthcare systems in Sub-Saharan Africa using local talent to combat the extreme shortage of healthcare professionals in underserved areas." Despite the fact that thirty-eight of the fifty-four countries in the region have one or more medical schools graduating health-care professionals each year, sub-Saharan health-care systems are among the most understaffed in the world. Chris told me, "They are not able to retain the people they train, so what we are doing is to support young professionals who are graduating so that they can stick around and serve their populations locally."

Once Chris identified brain drain as his vision's fundamental obstacle, the solution to create a two-year paid fellowship program for medical professionals became clear. As he explained in an interview with NPR, "The misconception is that a doctor who just graduated [and who is] highly talented [and] highly educated do[es]n't need any help. By thinking that way, we lose them because we can't compensate them or pay them enough to stay." Now all three products—the village ambulance, the mobile hospital, and the fellowship for health-care professionals in Africa—are part of Health Access Corps' work toward realizing Chris's vision of access to health care for every human being.

Chris has shown incredible determination throughout his whole life, from his early days fighting for his own survival to these more recent moments fighting for his vision to get quality health care to sub-Saharan Africa. His story fuels his own passion as well as that of others who have joined his movement—the staff, partners, and funders of Health Access Corps, among them Google, the United Nations Foundation, and Newman's Own Foundation. While Chris had to continually adapt his strategy, as his initial ideas didn't quite achieve what he wanted, each time he learned something new about *why* the current idea didn't work and how he should evolve it. By being so clear about his ultimate vision, he has been able to get closer to achieving it with each successive strategy.

THEORY OF CHANGE

ONCE YOU HAVE a compelling vision and the purpose behind it clearly articulated, the next step is to think about how to make it a reality—what steps will be required to spark and maintain that movement to get the result you want? In the world of social change organizations, nonprofits, and often in government, it is common to use a methodology called the Theory of Change as a means to maximize the chances of success for a desired change. This method involves starting with the goals you want to achieve and then identifying the necessary preconditions to reach those goals and the links between each outcome along the way. While it is typical in most organizations to set goals and use metrics to measure them, this approach is different. It specifically examines how the goals relate to the end result you are trying to achieve and how the goals relate to one another. With a Theory of Change, you focus on how one step in a process is a precondition for the next, starting with the result that you want and then working backward to determine the steps to get there. What are the things you need to do? Whom do you need to persuade? Is it believable that one step will lead to the next, and that by following those steps you can reach your goal? Put more simply, a Theory of Change is a hypothesis about the steps that will lead to your desired outcome: A + B + C = D.

As an example, petitions that are successful at Change.org each have a good Theory of Change. For petition starters, the vision or outcome they want to achieve depends on being able to persuade a specific decision-maker (elected official, corporate exec, etc.) who actually has the ability to make the desired change. So a good Theory of Change for a petition involves making sure you identify the right decision-maker, creating an ask that the decision-maker might be willing or even excited to agree to, and then outlining a compelling reason for them to do it. If you start with the results you want—your vision—you can work backward to the steps you need to take and the people you need to influence in order to make it happen. Each movement would have its own unique Theory of Change based on identifying the vision and the necessary preconditions for that outcome to occur.

Change.org as a company has a Theory of Change for how it intends to achieve its vision, which says:

- First *empower organizers* with the tools and support that enable anyone to start an effective campaign.
- These campaigns spread through compelling personal stories, and thereby *mobilize supporters* in massive numbers, who contribute their voices, time, and money.
- The scale of this mobilization helps to *engage decision-makers*, providing more incentives for them to listen and authentically respond.
- When people are more empowered to speak up, realizing the power of collective action, and decision-makers are more motivated to respond, you create a systemic shift in power and *transformative change* that can improve the world.

The elements of the Theory of Change build on each other. Each one is a precondition of the next. You can't effectively engage decision-makers without having enough mass mobilization to help them understand the importance of a given change; you can't mobilize large numbers of supporters unless you first empower people to come forward as organizers with something to mobilize people around, and so on.

The chart that follows is from the Center for Theory of Change, a nonprofit that promotes standards and best practices for implementing a Theory of Change. It shows a more detailed example from Project Superwomen, a collaboration of several organizations working toward a vision of a world where domestic violence survivors have stable, long-term employment at livable wages. They started at

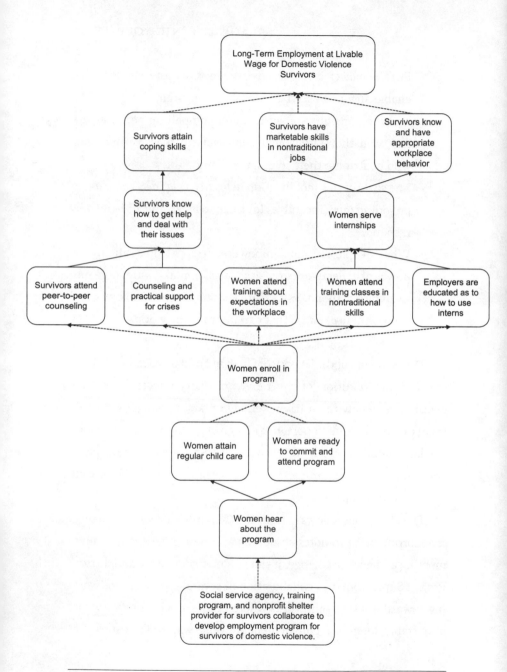

Sample Theory of Change from Project Superwomen

the top and worked backward, identifying the preconditions for each outcome.

You can imagine how a Theory of Change would work in a more traditional business as well. For instance, if Alli Webb at Drybar ultimately envisions a world where women can feel more confident every day because their hair looks great, then preconditions of her achieving that vision at scale might be the expansion into more locations, the development of products people can use at home, and training tools (like books and videos) that teach people how to style their hair on their own—all of which Drybar is currently doing.

There is more detail available about this process at the website of the Center for Theory of Change. Once you have created a clear Theory of Change—a road map for *how* you plan to achieve your vision—you can use it as a guide for what to prioritize, how to measure whether each step is working, and whether or not you are staying on track to achieve your goal.

KINDLING FOR YOUR FIRE

YOUR VISION AND purpose may be deeply personal, but ultimately, you need to attract passionate supporters to ensure that your movement takes off. Finding those first few people who can influence others to support you is a critical next step. If you view your own idea as the spark for your movement, then these early, influential supporters are the kindling for your fire. In his TED talk about starting movements, entrepreneur Derek Sivers illustrates this point with a video example of a lone man dancing energetically at a concert. As soon as a second person gets up to dance with him, others quickly follow. Sivers notes that you don't have a movement until you have your first followers—those courageous people who stand up to join you. How you find and treat those first followers is key to the ultimate success of your cause. Your first supporters are leaders, too, and they decide whether your movement takes off.

Megan at Yellowberry had success through an influential blog on Facebook that posted about her product. Alli Webb's first loyal clients supported her move to her initial physical location, and a post in the popular blog *DailyCandy* spiked interest in her business. Each of these movement starters used creativity and persistence to find the right influencers to spread the word and help their ideas catch fire.

Influencers are any individuals with a following of people who trust them; celebrities and journalists are obvious influencers, but coworkers, teachers, and even friends and family can be influencers if they can reach enough people. The statistics show just how persuasive influencers are: according to Nielsen, 92 percent of people trust recommendations from individuals—even if they don't know them—more than they trust other more traditional forms of advertising. Influencers exist in many different forms and are motivated by different things, so the key is to research and understand who might be the influencers in your category, your location, etc. Sometimes they are bloggers, YouTubers, or other online personalities with large followings. Sometimes they are members of the press, and sometimes they are the most influential people in a neighborhood or within an organization.

There is a growing industry around paid influencer marketing, yet there are many times when, especially for an important purpose, influencers will support a cause they believe in without expecting payment. The key is to make the influencers feel as though they are getting something of value in return for their promotion, whether that value is something of theirs you agree to promote in return (sometimes called "share for share"), getting early or free access to a product, or just being able to feel good that they made a positive difference in the world. Understanding and persuading influencers to support your movement can work using techniques similar to the ones we'll discuss in Chapter 4 about how to persuade decision-makers—the people with the power to make a change you are looking for.

Often, "micro-influencers," who have a strong and engaged relationship with a smaller set of relevant people, can be more effective at getting your message to the right audience than celebrities with huge followings, as Gretta Rose van Riel discovered. Gretta is a serial entrepreneur from Australia who had started several multimillion-dollar businesses before she was thirty, beginning with SkinnyMe Tea, which created the category of tea-based cleanses she calls "teatoxes." She's also a major influencer in her own right, often called "the Instagram queen" because she now has a combined following across her businesses of over 16 million people. Gretta believed that her product would advance her vision of creating an easy way for people to be healthier, and she wanted to reach young women like herself. She reached out to people on Instagram who fit her target audience and had over 1,000 followers, and sent them some free tea. It was remarkably effective. As Gretta described in an interview with *Influencive*, SkinnyMe Tea had grown to $600,000 per month in sales, just six months after Gretta founded the company. She says, "Back in 2012, one girl from Tasmania had 1000 followers, posted our tea and made the most sales we ever had in a day. After that, I'd screenshot every girl with over 1000 followers, and reach out to them with our tea. When we reached out to girls, they were so not used to being approached, 90–95% of influencers were stoked to do it. They weren't used to VIP treatment, no companies were sending out free stuff back then! We were one of the first brands, if not the first, to pursue influencer branding at the time."

It was such an effective model for Gretta that she was able to replicate it for several other businesses. Although she describes feeling like it was a fluke or just luck, she studied all the data she had about which of her strategies were working and uncovered how to replicate her success in spreading her movement. In a recent interview with *Foundr*, Gretta describes three techniques she believes work especially well for getting the most out of collaborating with influencers:

- **The Thunderclap**—Get large numbers of people to promote something in the same time frame, leading to a large amount of consolidated attention. You usually see this happen with people using the same hashtags at the same time. An additional benefit of the Thunderclap is that this synchronized approach can sometimes push a topic onto trending lists on social media sites, resulting in even more promotion.

- **The Trendsetter**—Identify both macro- and micro-influencers in the same cluster or topic area and target a macro-influencer first. The macro-influencer then encourages the micro-influencers' enthusiasm, compounding support.
- **Social Proof**—Get real people to post user-generated content about your product or cause. Even if they themselves are not influencers, getting large numbers of "regular" people to post and share can be a very effective strategy. Change.org works this way; the petition starter shares the campaign with his or her network, the people in their networks have a strong incentive to share it with their own networks, and so on.

• • •

UNDERSTANDING THE CHANNELS for social promotion that you have available is critical. Katherine Krug is the founder and CEO of BetterBack, a company that designs products to help ease lower back pain. She is the first solo female entrepreneur to raise over $1 million on Kickstarter for her business; now, she has raised more than $3 million on multiple crowdfunding sites. When she was first getting started, one key to her early success was understanding how the algorithms worked on Kickstarter so she could get her project featured in the "Most Popular" category. As she said in an interview with *Forbes,* "The North Star of any campaign should be getting into the Most Popular category so people browsing on the platform can see your project. The most important factor in the Most Popular algorithm is the number of backers, NOT dollars raised, over a given period." So Katherine e-mailed 120 of her friends asking if they would each be willing to give one dollar on the day of the launch. This strategy, similar to Gretta's Thunderclap technique, paid off. On its launch day, BetterBack made it to the Most Popular category. Katherine has maintained momentum long after launch by rigorously looking at the data, watching which messages and calls to action are most effective.

Katherine built her movement through crowdfunding because it gave her direct access to her customers and supporters. As she told *Forbes*, "Crowdfunding has democratized access to capital and removed all the gatekeepers. There is not a room full of men to pitch to." Instead, she said, "the only people you have to pitch and satisfy are your future customers." If you choose this approach, make sure you take good care of those supporters to keep the movement going. Katherine provides regular updates about her project, giving backers access to upgrades and discounts, and quickly responds to their questions. "Your backers are literally bringing your dream to life," she told *Forbes*, "so think about how you can add value through every single interaction."

FOLLOWERS BECOME LEADERS

JENNIFER CARDENAS GREW up the daughter of a single mom, fiercely self-sufficient, often taking care of her younger sister, and with the desire to always be the responsible one. She has spent her whole life in two small towns outside Houston, right in the epicenter of where Hurricane Harvey hit in 2017. She and her family had originally planned to stay in their home during the storm, having lived through other hurricanes. But when a mandatory evacuation was ordered, Jennifer and her family left home in a rush at the last possible moment.

As they drove toward San Antonio, Jennifer saw many of her friends posting on Facebook about where they were evacuating, so she decided to create a Facebook group so they could keep track of where everyone was, and whether they were safe or needed help. She called it "Hurricane Harvey 2017." She wrote to her friends: "Hey guys, I made this group so I can keep in touch with you all, and you can all keep in touch with me. I can only add 50 people right now, I'm in a hurry, but I'll add some more people later. You are all free to add your family and friends so everyone can keep in touch. Bye." And then she went to dinner with her family. When she looked back at the group later that evening, 800 people had asked to join.

The group grew exponentially; the next day there were 30,000 members, and within four days, more than 150,000. Jennifer reached out to her sister, Shanna Lyons, in Maryland, to help, since she knew she couldn't manage it all on her own. And then something magical happened—people from all around the country and the world started offering their expertise. People who had lived through similar experiences posted live videos with advice for how to survive a large storm, one woman offered a spreadsheet she had used to coordinate previous disasters, and other people offered help to Jennifer and her sister by serving as moderators of the group, facilitators of rescues, and more. Though Jennifer had started the group and had been its initial leader, her first supporters became leaders in their own right.

And these volunteer leaders were critical to the success of the group. When Jennifer drove back to her hometown of Ingleside, Texas, the day after the storm, she had trouble getting Internet service for the next several days. And the group kept going, even without her online. Jennifer says that when she was finally able to get service, she couldn't believe what was happening. "I started seeing the rescues," she told me. "People were posting 'Please help, I'm on my roof.' And then I would see 'Rescued.' And I had all of these messages that said things like, 'Oh my god, you have saved so many lives. Thank you for what you've done.'" She called her sister to find out what was happening, and Shanna said, "Jennifer, it's incredible what's happening. We are conducting rescues, we have dispatch teams, we have rescue teams. We're coordinating with Coast Guard and National Guard and local and state services and agencies, and lives are being saved. It's an amazing thing."

People unified around the common purpose of the group, and they all wanted to be a part of it; there were eighty volunteer moderators who took leadership roles in the community and thousands more who lent a helping hand however they could. They took over where Jennifer had started. Working together with first responders, Jennifer's Facebook community was responsible for rescuing more than eight thousand people during Hurricane Harvey. The community is still active, though its purpose has evolved. Now it helps people manage the complex and emotional process of rebuilding: navigating FEMA, providing advice on how to rebuild homes, coordinating clothing and furniture donations, and anything else that other members need. It may take years to recover, and Jennifer's community will continue to play an important role.

• • •

THE WORK YOU do to create a clear and compelling vision—of articulating and refining what you want to create and why—will pay off when starting your movement. Once you have a sharp and focused view of your desired future, you can then successfully motivate and inspire others to join you.

4

GET TO KNOW GOLIATH

Persuading decision-makers

Don't raise your voice; improve your argument.

—Desmond Tutu

RETHINKING DAVID AND GOLIATH

THE WORLD OF traditional social organizing frequently calls upon the David versus Goliath paradigm. As we discussed in Chapter 3, most campaigns involve a decision-maker, a person or group of people that has the power to make the change you want. Decision-makers are usually elected officials or heads of organizations. It is common for activists to refer to the decision-makers they are trying to persuade as "targets" and to think about how to get those targets to agree to change through virtually any legal means necessary, including sometimes problematic tactics like "twitter bombing" that are specifically meant to shame and harass a decision-maker. I believe, however, that social organizers could benefit from a more collaborative approach that business leaders often use in an effort to get longer-term wins.

Instead of viewing people in power as targets and using any means at our disposal to get a short-term win, what if we see them as potential long-term partners? To build those long-term partnerships, we must choose tactics that encourage decision-makers to work more productively with us, *both* in the current campaign and in future ones. Some might suggest that's not possible because decision-makers have so much power that it's impossible for the "little people" to persuade them unless we fight fire with fire. I disagree. I believe that there is far more power in the collective mobilization of citizens than in any one given decision-maker, as long as we can find the right tools to communicate with each other.

For individuals, the key is in understanding our own strength. We have to know where our power lies and realize that when we work together effectively, it is nearly impossible for decision-makers not to listen. I'm not suggesting that people avoid traditional organizing tactics—strategies like peaceful demonstrations, petitions, boycotts, lawsuits, and even flooding decision-makers with emails, letters, phone calls, and social media can all be extremely effective ways to let them know that we are passionate about a given issue. I am suggesting that *when* we employ tactics like those, we consider doing them respectfully, leaving open the possibility of a positive interaction rather than shaming, harassing, or embarrassing someone.

Dr. Martin Luther King Jr.'s nonviolent approach, based on the teachings of Gandhi, kept this core principle in mind. Dr. King's six principles of nonviolence aren't simply about not becoming violent. Rather, they're about practicing love over hate and about seeking a path toward long-term understanding as a tool for justice. The third principle, "Nonviolence seeks to defeat injustice, not people," recognizes that "evildoers are also victims and are not evil people." By seeking to understand them, we can ultimately have a better chance at establishing justice long-term.

As we watch and respond to the rise of the "alt-right" and the growing confidence of hate groups around the world, the principles of nonviolence remain as relevant today as they were during the civil rights movement. And while the pillars of nonviolence provide useful guidelines for how to react in isolated incidents like counter-protests, they can also steer long-term strategy about how to work with decision-makers. After all, although they don't always behave that way, nearly all decision-makers are in roles that are *in service* to people, whether their constituents, their employees, their students, their customers, or their shareholders. Remind them that it is in their best interest to actually serve.

While working to persuade decision-makers, remember that you have more power than you may think. While we commonly use the story of David and Goliath to describe a situation in which a seemingly weaker opponent faces a much stronger one, *New Yorker* writer Malcolm Gladwell suggests in his book *David and Goliath* that we may have the David and Goliath story all wrong. Gladwell writes that there is strength in being the underdog: "The fact of being an underdog can change people in ways that we often fail to appreciate. It can open doors and create opportunities and make possible what might otherwise have seemed unthinkable."

In fact, we may have misinterpreted that story altogether,

Gladwell argues, citing medical experts who believe that Goliath was so large due to a condition caused by a benign pituitary tumor. Despite his gargantuan size, the tumor may have blinded him and slowed him down, rendering him a significantly less threatening opponent. As Gladwell says, "What the Israelites saw, from high on the ridge, was an intimidating giant. In reality, the very thing that gave the giant his size was also the source of his greatest weakness. There is an important lesson in that for battles with all kinds of giants. The powerful and the strong are not always what they seem."

We can make change happen by reframing decision-makers as potential long-term partners and trying to understand their motivations. If we remember that decision-makers, for the most part, are also good people whose actions are driven by their own incentives and sense of purpose, then it's more effective to make change by helping both sides win. Finding ways to work collaboratively with a decision-maker today may lead to a much bigger long-term payoff, as that person will remain open to working with us again.

The social-organizing world often refers to a classic image of many small fish coming together to chase a big fish. I'm suggesting a twist: the many small fish still organize to show the power in numbers, but they first try to work with the big fish, chasing it only when it's absolutely necessary. In many cases it may not be.

I realize this may seem naive to some, and I know there are certainly parts of the world where even peacefully speaking up can put people at risk of arrest or physical harm. And there are cases of extremely difficult decision-makers—fascist dictators, people who are prone to violence or not at all interested in dialogue or reason,

Current Organizing Model

Proposed Organizing Model

etc.—with whom this type of approach may not work at all. But I believe that in more situations than you'd expect, a strategy that aligns the interests of apparent "opponents" gets superior results.

Most of us have the same core needs and emotions: the need for physical safety and financial security, the hunger for love and approval, the desire to do well at whatever we take on. That means that there is common ground between people who want to drive change and the decision-makers they depend on to do so. If each side tries to understand the motivations of the other, then as in any negotiation, the outcome will be better. And as someone who has been both "David" and "Goliath," I know it is easier to listen and respond to people agitating for change when you feel you are being approached as a person rather than David to Goliath or "us against them."

So yes, I believe we can get to a world where David and Goliath are both winners. There are already so many examples where this is the case, several of which are highlighted in this chapter. We can do it if we work with our voices, our conviction, and our power in numbers. We can do it if we express our purpose and vision from one human being to another and put away our slingshots rather than continue to hurl rocks at Goliath. (Okay, seemingly naive rant over.)

IDENTIFY THE RIGHT DECISION-MAKER

PART OF DEVELOPING any good Theory of Change is understanding which specific person has the ability to make the change you want, no matter what it is. It could be launching a new program at your workplace or school, funding a new company you are starting, changing a policy or law in your city or country, or even just getting your first few influencers on board. Whatever you are trying to accomplish, there is usually a particular person or group of people that has the ability or the power to make that happen. This person or group is your decision-maker.

Before you think through the tactics to persuade your decision-maker, it's critical to make sure you have in fact identified the right person or people. If you want to change the rules about parking tickets in your town, you don't ask the president of the country. You'd be surprised how many petitions around almost any topic are directed at the president—truly amazing. Or sometimes people direct their campaigns to generic decision-makers, like "the people of earth." Good luck getting the people of earth to coordinate on just about anything.

Being clear about whom you need to persuade is a key part of achieving your goal. Sometimes desired changes can be tackled from different angles that would each have a different decision-maker. For instance, if you want a particular grocery store to stop using plastic bags, you could identify the company itself as a decision-maker, or the legislature of that city or state to try to get them to pass a law that prevents the use of plastic bags, like several U.S. cities have done, or charges for single-use plastic bags the way the United Kingdom has done.

Once you identify the who—the right decision-maker—you'll need to determine the what: a realistic ask for a decision-maker to agree to. The what needs to be something that person can actually do. If you are trying to get someone pardoned for a crime, if it is a federal crime, then the president *could* do it. If it is a state crime, the president could not do that, even if he or she wanted to. It's not enough to just want change. You have to also find a pathway to change that is accessible to both sides. The real magic comes when you can find a way to make the change appealing to the decision-maker as well.

UNDERSTAND GOLIATH

ONE WAY TO break down the walls between you and Goliath and successfully persuade decision-makers to act is to try to understand them and learn what motivates them; Goliath has needs, too. This is similar to the technique we'll discuss in Chapter 5, inspiring supporters—the better you understand what motivates people, the more easily you can inspire them to take action.

Gemma Mortensen, former chief global officer at Change.org and executive director at Crisis Action, had recently started in her role at Crisis Action when it helped organize an emergency response to the violent crackdown on Myanmar's Buddhist monks in 2007. The country had seen enormous violence against peaceful protestors and the arrest of many political prisoners, and there was an eruption of spontaneous outrage and concern around the world. Crisis Action was able to bring together a coalition of NGOs, activists, trade unions, celebrities, and faith leaders to demonstrate the strength of public support for the issue. Their goal was to get the European Union to put in place economic sanctions and for the United Nations Security Council (UNSC) to take action on Myanmar, which had never happened before.

They knew that Gordon Brown, the prime minister of the United Kingdom at the time, cared greatly about Myanmar. Conversations with his key aides made it clear that he was ready to take real leadership of the crisis and push for action, creating an opportunity for activists and decision-makers to join forces. As Gemma explained to me, "Rather than seeing all those in power as the problem, we understood that if you engage in the right way, you can help shift political momentum much faster than if you are just antagonistic. Gordon Brown was prepared to show real leadership on this; he was prepared to do the right thing. So we said, 'If we help people get out on the streets on this, what will you do?' His team said he would come out personally and say, 'I am going to the United Nations Security Council to say this must be the moment where finally we take action on Burma.'"

So on the morning of the global marches Crisis Action coordinated, they organized senior Burmese Buddhist monks, heads of the Trades Union Congress and Amnesty International, and former political prisoners from Myanmar who had extraordinary personal stories to meet the prime minister. It was a very moving meeting.

On October 6, 2007, as thousands of people marched through the streets of London, Gordon Brown spoke publicly, telling the delegation: "I want the EU to impose further sanctions on the regime to make it absolutely clear we will not tolerate the abuses that have taken place.

"I want all the other leaders of the world to work with us to achieve the progress that all of you here want . . . an end to abuse of human rights, we want the violence to stop against the people of Burma and we want to move forward with the process of democracy and reconciliation as soon as possible."

For Gemma, who had been working to change the world most of her life, this was one of those incredible moments in which the path to progress became clear. If you understand your decision-maker, the political context in which they have to operate, and what motivates them, you can work collaboratively and effectively to solve a problem together.

And just a few days later, on October 11, the UNSC took its first ever action on Myanmar, issuing a presidential statement condemning the violence against peaceful demonstrators and calling for the early release of all political prisoners. On October 15, the European Union banned imports of timber, metals, and gems from Myanmar and threatened a ban on all new investment if the government did not enter into genuine dialogue with the democracy movement. These were big steps. And while it took time for major change to happen, this was a critical piece of the puzzle.

As Gemma made clear, no one organization or individual can claim credit for big developments in social change. It is always the collective effort of many people—whether activists, decision-makers, businesses, or others—who help make change. And it is often work that continues for many years; though Myanmar has undergone a dramatic political transition, activists are still striving to secure the protection of minorities, such as the Rohingya Muslim community, from violent persecution.

DRAW THE MAP

ORGANIZERS USE A technique called "power mapping" or "influence mapping" to formalize the process that Gemma outlines. It asks you to understand the spheres of relationships and motivators that influence your decision-maker. This is often a visual exercise in which people quite literally map out—draw, list, diagram—how they might be able to sway a decision-maker toward action. If you understand the people, institutions, and processes that motivate and influence someone, then you are better equipped to persuade them.

As you go through this exercise, it's important to clearly understand and denote any relationships between the people on your map. How many connections are there between key people, and how strong are those connections? How likely would each of those people or institutions be to support your idea? Are there primary and secondary decision-makers, and if so, how are they related? Are there any smaller asks you can start with that will help build to the bigger and final ask? This process will also help you clarify the order in which you approach people to get to the ultimate decision-maker, starting with the strongest connections and those most likely to support your idea.

To truly understand the effects of power mapping, consider this example. Throughout 2012, a campaign to end the Boy Scouts of America's (BSA) ban on gay Scouts and gay Scout leaders built momentum on Change.org. In April 2012, Jennifer Tyrrell, who had served for a year as den leader of her son's Cub Scout pack in Ohio, was removed from this position and had her BSA membership revoked because she was gay. Soon afterward, and with the support of GLAAD, she launched a petition on Change.org asking the BSA to end this discriminatory policy. She and her supporters knew that they were facing an uphill battle. The Boy Scouts of America is a century-old institution that is not known for changing its policies. So Jennifer and others in her movement began to look at other ways they might be able to persuade the BSA to change, beginning with a thorough review of the various people and institutions that had influence on the actions of the BSA.

They started with the BSA's board of directors, which included a host of Fortune 500 CEOs, several of whom led companies like AT&T and Ernst & Young that were at the forefront of the fight for LGBTQ rights. Jennifer launched an additional petition directed to AT&T and Ernst & Young asking their CEOs to speak out in favor of changing the policy, and both of them did. Next, the team looked at corporations that had partnerships with the Boy Scouts of America. From there, they homed in on the companies that had the best record on LGBTQ rights according to the Human Rights Campaign's Corporate Equality Index. That led to petitions asking companies like Intel, UPS, and others to speak out about the Boy Scouts' ban on gay Scouts and leaders. All the companies did.

In addition to leveraging the voices of companies and corporate leaders, the team also asked famous celebrities, politicians, and other notable figures with ties to the Boy Scouts to speak out on social media in favor of changing the policy. They persuaded musicians like Carly Rae Jepsen and Train not to perform at a concert at the Boy Scout Jamboree, a very large national conference of Boy Scouts held every four years.

Lastly, they mapped out the national and local structure of the BSA. As they learned, the BSA is composed of a number of local Scout councils all throughout the United States. They leveraged every part of the power map by helping to launch 110 petitions on Change.org, urging the councils to ask the national organization to end their ban on gay Scouts and leaders. Each petition was started by someone who cared about this issue and had some personal connection to it— including gay people who themselves had been Scouts or leaders or who had gay parents who were Scout leaders—demonstrating the size and diversity of the community that cared about this issue.

All of these additional campaigns with smaller asks were directed toward people and institutions within the influence map of the BSA and helped to create an incredible wave of momentum and media attention. Finally, just over a year after the initial petition was launched, the BSA voted to end the ban on gay Scouts on May 23, 2013. And two years later, in July 2015, the BSA also lifted its ban on gay Scout leaders. In the end, no single campaign changed the minds of the BSA. Instead, the movement succeeded because of the coordinated efforts of more than one hundred smaller, related campaigns, each directed at people within the BSA's spheres of influence. What had started as a single campaign directed at the BSA grew into a national movement with nearly 1.5 million supporters.

The movement created a win-win. It made sense for the BSA to listen to and engage with the people who were asking them for change, and in the end, the change they made was also likely better for the long-term success of their organization. Public opinion shifted dramatically in favor of gay rights during those years, followed by a wave of legal reforms as twenty-five states voted in favor of same-sex marriage in 2013 and 2014. In 2015, the U.S. Supreme Court ruled that banning same-sex marriage was unconstitutional. Given this change in perspective, the BSA's new policy ultimately put them on the side of public opinion as well, a positive outcome for their organization and for the people who were proposing the change.

•   •   •

ANOTHER EXAMPLE OF someone who deeply understands how to influence decision-makers is my friend Luanne Calvert, who spent five years as CMO of Virgin America airlines. Luanne is one of the most creative people I've ever met, and her talent has clearly contributed to her extremely successful career in advertising and marketing. During her time at Yahoo!, Google, Virgin, and several other companies, Luanne has been responsible for a lot of firsts—the first ever "buzz" or word-of-mouth marketing team, the first Internet-enabled taxis (before there was mobile Internet or Uber), and on and on—meaning that she has also become an incredible expert at persuading people to do things that they might at first be hesitant to do.

One of my favorite examples of a Luanne "first" is when she led the effort to create the now-famous musical safety video at Virgin

America. She describes it as a "gut-wrenching" experience because, although people may not remember now, the previous safety video, which was a humorous animation, was beloved by Virgin America customers and very much served to define their brand. To come up with something that their passionate customers would like better, or even as much, was an enormously high bar to reach. Luanne needed to create a movement of her own within Virgin America—one that her colleagues would get behind, even if it was risky. Despite having done so many creative things in her career, she was scared to make this change. She didn't want to be the person who ruined the brand, because everyone loved that animated video. Ultimately they had to make a change. The animation didn't meet the standards for addressing the hearing-impaired audience, and the FAA was going to fine them if she didn't change it.

So she took a leap, reached out to her colleagues at Virgin Produced, and told them she wanted to do something that "had never been done before"—one of Luanne's favorite phrases. What they came up with was amazing and surprised even Luanne. "They said they wanted to do an homage to music, because Virgin has a history of music," she told me, "and we want to do the first ever completely rhyming music safety video." Luanne thought that idea sounded perfect. They hired Jon Chu, who had directed Justin Bieber's documentary and *Step Up 2*, among other popular films, and got started.

To get the video up and running, though, Luanne had to get through a gauntlet of decision-makers who all had opinions. Rather than let that deter her, Luanne did something unusual. Instead of just thinking about primary decision-makers whose approval she required, like the CEO (her boss) and the FAA (who came to the video shoot to make sure everything was in compliance), she actually expanded her outreach to people whose input and buy-in would be helpful for her to get. This meant showing it to everyone—from other executives to flight attendants who would have to hear it every day to loyal frequent flyers.

One person whose input she had sought ended up being critical in the ultimate approval process. When Luanne met with the CEO, he was hesitant about the music, thinking it might get annoying to people over time. In that meeting, a new colleague of Luanne's, their chief pilot and COO, Steve Forte, spoke up in favor of the video. He said, "I love it. The more you hear it, the more you love it." Broadening the outreach to a wider set of initial decision-makers may have been the turning point in getting the ultimate approval. Reaching out to a broader set of people also helped ensure the video's successful launch, because she was confident that customers would like it.

And in classic Luanne style, Virgin America launched the new safety video just as you would promote a new movie—Jon Chu went on *The Ellen DeGeneres Show*, and they played the video in Times Square at an event with flight attendants. And it was a huge success, even more loved than the original animated video. So much so, in fact, that some of their flight attendants started dancing to it—and a passenger-filmed video went viral, creating even more attention for the brand.

Though it may seem like a small detail, the safety video had a massive impact on the movement that Virgin America was creating with their brand. (Note: Alaska Airlines acquired Virgin America in 2016 and may discontinue the Virgin America brand by 2019.) As Luanne told me, "What I love about it in the end is that it showed that you can take the most mundane things and create them into details that help to create a brand that people love."

RELEVANT VOICES MATTER

TESSA HILL AND Lia Valente were no strangers to sexism and harassment, even at age thirteen. Growing up in Ontario, Canada, they had heard stories from their friends about catcalling and slut shaming in the hallways at school and on social media. They'd learned from older siblings and the media about "rape culture," especially common on college campuses, where sexual assault is rarely punished and where survivors of all genders are often disregarded or even seen as at fault.

So when asked to choose a social justice topic they cared about for an eighth grade school project in 2014, they chose to tackle rape culture. Lia and Tessa started by filming their own documentary, *Allegedly*, which was not only viewed in their class but also featured on the *Huffington Post* and seen by nearly ten thousand people on YouTube. Then they created a Change.org petition called "We Give Consent" to fight for the concept of consent to be added to the sex education curriculum in their province, Ontario. More than forty thousand people signed the petition and left comments with their reasons for signing that ranged from their roles as parents to their perspectives as survivors to their admiration for Lia and Tessa. Though the reasons behind them differed, every signature and comment helped Tessa and Lia build meaningful support for their movement.

The passion and resolve of Tessa, Lia, and their forty thousand supporters garnered media coverage in outlets ranging from the *Toronto Star* to NPR to the major radio news show *Metro Morning* on CBC (the Canadian Broadcasting Corporation). Local coverage snowballed into national interest and captured the attention of the Ontario government. In fact, after the young women were interviewed on *Metro Morning*, Kathleen Wynne, the premier of Ontario, tweeted at Tessa and Lia that she wanted to meet with them.

Premier Wynne was inspired by these two young women who took action to further a purpose they believed in. The fact that they were students who would be participating in the revised curriculum mattered a lot to her. Their voices carried extra weight. And because the concept of consent was so important to them as young people, it, too, carried extra weight. Premier Wynne even told Lia and Tessa when they met that they reminded her of her own activism as a young woman, when she successfully persuaded her high school to change the dress code to let girls wear pants. Premier Wynne did decide to include the concept of consent as part of a curriculum change for all Ontario schools—thanks to Tessa and Lia. If an issue matters to you in an area where your voice has extra relevance, don't hesitate to speak up.

IF YOU DON'T ASK, YOU DON'T GET

SAIRA RAO AND Carey Albertine are the founders of In This Together Media, a company that creates children's books that highlight diversity in terms of race, gender, class, sexual orientation, and
experience. As they worked together to get the business off the
ground, Saira remembered a phrase an ex-boyfriend of hers used to
say: "If you don't ask, you don't get." She described to me how they
put that strategy to use effectively in the early days of growing their
business, when they were launching their first book series in early
2012. The series was called Soccer Sisters, and the launch coincided
with the 2012 Summer Olympics. Saira explained how they developed a great idea to get influencers on board, telling me, "Brandi
Chastain was going to be working for NBC covering the Olympics,
and we were sitting around a table laughing, 'Oh my God, wouldn't
it great if Brandi Chastain or Mia Hamm would be the spokesper-
son for this series?' We had no money. We had no track record. We
had just started."

Saira and Carey took a risk and e-mailed both women's managers. Brandi's manager responded quickly with a surprising answer:
"Brandi normally charges quite a bit of money for this, but she loves
what you're doing so she's going to do it for free." Carey and Saira
were thrilled. That first big risk led to appearances for Brandi on the
Today show to discuss the books, and to their first foreign rights
deals selling the books in Japan. Saira told me it made them completely rethink their strategy moving forward, making them realize

that "whoever it is that we're going to go after, we're going to go after. And we're not going to think about it. We're just going to ask everybody we know to help, and people have really risen to the occasion. It's been really encouraging."

There are times when it makes sense to just go for it and not overthink your strategy. Sometimes persuading a decision-maker just takes a well-placed ask.

MAKE IT EASY TO SAY YES

ONCE YOU UNDERSTAND who and what motivates your decision-makers, it also becomes easier to craft a plan that will get them to yes. One of the ways that people struggle most in working effectively with decision-makers is not knowing how to put the ask together in a way that makes it easy for them to agree. The advice I heard over and over again from activists and entrepreneurs I spoke to was how important it is to prepare carefully, do your research, and get ready for every potential scenario. Anticipating all the various reasons decision-makers might say no and what questions they might ask helps ensure that every possible base is covered when making your case.

One incredible example of getting people to yes is Amanda Nguyen, an astronaut-in-training and the founder of Rise, an organization that advocates for the legal protection of sexual assault survivors. Rise originated in Amanda's traumatic personal story: when she was a twenty-two-year-old college student at Harvard, she was raped. Within twenty-four hours of the assault, she did exactly what she was supposed to do, going to the hospital to have a rape kit examination. Even though she took immediate action, there was no guarantee that the critical evidence would be preserved long enough to be of use. That's because Massachusetts, where she was living at the time, keeps rape kits in evidence labs for only six months. What this means is that every six months, survivors have to fight to keep their critical evidence from the trash.

When Amanda took a closer look at the laws that aim to protect victims of sexual violence, she found a truly broken system. As she told me during a recent interview, "Fighting for the civil rights of rape survivors started from a very personal place. I remember walking out of the hospital and feeling so alone. People tell survivors to go to the criminal justice system, go get help. But when I went to try to get help, I was met with a legal labyrinth. It's quite retraumatizing to have to go through this continually and to fight to hold on to critical evidence in a violent crime—in my own rape—when other crimes are not treated this way. That's why it is a civil rights issue. Evidence for other crimes is stored indefinitely. You wouldn't throw away evidence in a murder case; why would you destroy evidence in a rape case? That's where I started researching what my rights were and decided to try to rewrite the law."

Amanda realized that in addition to trying to preserve the evidence in her own case, she wanted to do something on a bigger scale to protect other women from having their untested rape kits destroyed. She knew that she'd need help, so she reached out to a diverse group of friends and colleagues. By gathering this diverse set of experts, she was able to effectively anticipate the potential concerns that lawmakers might have. Not only did they prepare for questions that might be asked by members of Congress, but they also drafted a version of the bill so that the required work would be done for them.

Her networks and her friends were young professionals and law students, so Amanda combined their expertise. They had working sessions where people from different professional backgrounds would sit together and do research. They untangled the complicated and patchwork laws to learn which rights exist in each state. And what they came up with was a list of best practices that were uncontroversial, had legal precedents, and worked across states. The Rise team also used financial metrics to show how effective the bill was, showing economic projections of how this would help districts not only morally but also fiscally. "By the time that we presented this to members of the U.S. Congress, we had a solid ask," Amanda told me. "We had data behind it. And we had a prepared package of the bill. We had the bill language. Obviously it was amended as the process went on. But we came in with everything prepared. And any question that a Senator or member of Congress had, we would turn that memo around in a day because we were very solid on what our research was and what we were fighting for."

And they won. They drafted a law called the Sexual Assault Survivors' Rights Act (otherwise known as the Sexual Assault Survivors' Bill of Rights). It passed first in Massachusetts, where survivors no longer have to worry that the valuable evidence in their rape kits will be destroyed after six months, and then unanimously in Congress on October 7, 2016. *Let me repeat that*—the House and Senate passed this law *unanimously* during one of the most polarized, partisan times in our history. Since 1989, only twenty-one bills—0.016 percent of all bills—have passed unanimously in both chambers of Congress. It's an extremely rare occurrence and an exceptional accomplishment for anyone, not to mention a young woman in her twenties who is not a professional lobbyist.

BRING YOUR DATA (AND YOUR CAPE)

IN 2002, THREE years into my job at Yahoo!, I was given the opportunity to join a small "tiger team" of people working with Jeff Weiner (who later became the CEO of LinkedIn) to reinvent Yahoo! Search. We knew we were falling behind. In the early years, consumers had thought of Yahoo! as a search engine. But by 2002, most people saw Yahoo! as a "portal" and were using Google for search. My job was to lead marketing for Yahoo! Search, which meant first getting a deep understanding of consumer needs to inform product development, and then running a marketing campaign to tell people about the new product once it was ready, with the objective of increasing market share of people using Yahoo! Search.

It was a really exciting time. I vividly remember, after weeks of focus groups, having a conversation with Qi Lu (who then was head of engineering for Yahoo! Search and went on to top positions at Microsoft and Chinese search leader Baidu) in which I told him that we had a really clear view of what people wanted in search: to get the answers to their questions as quickly as possible, and without extra steps. They essentially wanted shortcuts. And in that moment, Qi looked at me and said, "Great, I can build that." Right then and there we envisioned a new Yahoo! Search that would give people the answers to their questions right on the search page itself. Whether they searched for weather, sports scores, stock quotes, or movie times, if we had the information, we'd provide it directly on the page, in addition to letting people also click out to other sites if they preferred. So we set out to rebuild the product and develop a marketing campaign for the new Yahoo! Search, with the tagline "The Shortcut to What You Want." (This change seems really obvious now because all search engines do it, but at the time, it was a big innovation.)

We began to develop different ideas for the marketing campaign, and we had what was considered to be a sizable budget by tech company standards (though it would seem very small to most consumer marketers). A lot of my time was spent running our findings and plans by executives because the strategy for Yahoo! Search was very important for the company.

There was one senior executive who was not in favor of our doing brand marketing. It wasn't that he disagreed with the specifics of the creative or the copy—he just didn't believe we needed to market it at all. He thought that while common in consumer goods, most tech companies didn't use brand marketing techniques and didn't need to. (Note: That was truer in the early days of the Internet, though Yahoo! was an exception even then, running TV ads with the iconic yodel that helped cement the brand. Today traditional marketing campaigns are common in tech, and everyone from Google to Amazon does classic brand marketing.) Given what I knew was his strong disapproval, I was scared to present to him. Looking back, it seems silly to have been scared, but I was. I had seen him sometimes be critical or condescending to people in meetings, and I couldn't help thinking about how he would react.

Several months later, after we had run the full campaign, including print, digital, and television ads, I needed to present the results of our marketing efforts to him. As I was preparing for it over the weekend, I visited my parents and saw my father's cousin Bill Oberfield, who was also in town and who happens to be a psychiatrist. When Bill asked me how work was going, I explained how nervous I was about the looming presentation.

What he said next stayed with me: "What if you imagined yourself as a superhero in an action movie. Imagine that there's a crowd of people and they're all right behind you, cheering you on. When you walk into that meeting, imagine you're wearing a superhero cape. If he says something that knocks you off guard, take a deep breath, imagine your cape, and imagine the audience rooting for you."

At the time I thought it was a super-cheesy suggestion, but you bet I went to that meeting wearing bright red, thinking: "I'm going into this meeting like a superhero badass, and I'm imagining my cape. Whatever he says, I'll just take a deep breath and keep going."

I walked into the meeting, and before I could start the presentation, he opened the conversation by saying, "I don't know what you're about to present, but all I know is we spent way too much money on this campaign; it didn't work and I'll never do it again."

Talk about a rough way to start a meeting.

It was a damn good thing I had brought that imaginary cape. And I brought one other key item to that meeting—*indisputable data*. Turns out that's pretty powerful as well. So as I'd been coached, I took a deep breath and said, "Okay, I understand that you feel that way. Why don't I take you through the data anyway?"

As we started going through the deck, something dramatic happened. It became clear that our data was irrefutable. One slide in particular showed a clear representation of the market share of Yahoo! Search before our ad campaign started and immediately after our ad campaign ran. We had gained a full point of market share, which was worth many tens of millions of dollars to the company. It was clear that, regardless of anyone's opinion, the data told the truth. We went through the rest of the deck, and at the end of the presentation, he looked me in the eye and said, "You know what? You have the data and you showed me that I was wrong; this was actually a good campaign." It was a complete turnaround.

I realized two key things in that moment. First, I had more power than I thought, and data can be a meaningful equalizer. The combination of hard facts and more confidence in myself meant that I was able to be on a level playing field with someone I previously saw as intimidating. Second, I didn't need to see us as hero and antagonist (or David and Goliath) at all. Ultimately, we were on the same team (and in this case, we were *literally* on the same team—working for the same company and with the same objective). It was so early in my career that I didn't understand what it feels like to sit in the decision-maker seat—the one who has to make the calls about what to approve and not approve in the budget, risking the company's resources for things that may or may not work. Now that I do that on a regular basis, I realize how much pressure it is. And if I had tried to understand that more at the time, I might have been able to arm him with more information to feel better about the decision to begin with, or to admit that I also saw potential risks in the approach so we could try to work through them together.

We ultimately built a good relationship over time based on mutual respect, and we are still in touch. And while that experience taught me a lot about better preparing the decision-makers I work with for big decisions I am asking them to make, I also learned about the courage it takes as a decision-maker to admit when you are wrong about something. I admire him for that and try to remember the benefits of doing that myself.

Clear data can help to persuade even the most skeptical decision-makers and can help you build a relationship up front so that you can empower them to have the information they need to make a good decision and to see where it might benefit them. Data gives you power. And if you can't get far enough with just the data, you might want to throw on your cape.

TAKE THE LONG VIEW

ONE THING TO keep in mind is how long some of these movements can take—even when the idea has a tremendous amount of support at the outset—and how having patience with the process can really pay off. It took eight years for a group of concerned parents from the Down Syndrome Association of Northern Virginia who talked around a kitchen table in 2006 about the need for individuals with disabilities and their families to plan for their financial futures. Their advocacy, with the help of Sara Weir, the president of the National Down Syndrome Society (NDSS), and an extraordinary young woman with Down syndrome herself, Sara Wolff, the campaign's spokeswoman, would lead to the creation of the Achieving a Better Life Experience (ABLE) Act of 2013. ABLE accounts are tax-advantaged savings accounts that allow people with disabilities to save up to $100,000 without risking their eligibility for government programs like Social Security and Medicare or Medicaid. (The previous savings limit was only $2,000, which made it extremely difficult for people with disabilities or their families to save for their future.) The ABLE Act is considered the broadest piece of public policy legislation benefiting disabled Americans since the Americans with Disabilities Act (ADA). It acknowledges and provides assistance to 58 million people, helping them afford accessible housing and transportation, assistive technology, and additional health-care services not covered by insurance.

Sara Weir related to me the many steps and stages involved in pushing the bill forward—which took over eight years and spanned five U.S. Congresses. She and her supporters set up an ambassador program that was made up of advocates whose phone calls, e-mails, and personal stories helped get the attention of Washington lawmakers; they created a bipartisan collaborative approach to congressional leaders that resulted in an unprecedented 380 members of Congress cosponsoring the bill. (That is particularly unusual for a spending bill like this one.) Although the initial process was slow, taking the time to build up these relationships and make sure legislators really understood the issue benefited NDSS enormously.

Though it took eight years to get the initial bill passed into law, it took only seven more months to get related ABLE laws passed in *forty-seven of fifty states*. Because they took the long view, they were able to work productively with members from both sides of the aisle in achieving the outcome they wanted: "I don't think at any point in time during this decade-long journey did we ever take a contentious approach to anything related to the ABLE Act," she told me. "Our greatest challenge in getting to as many elected officials as we could was to really educate them—because when you say that somebody with a disability can't have more than $2,000, chins hit the table. Eyes get wide. People ask, 'How is that possible? How is that even a reality? And why hasn't that changed over the course of the last almost sixty years?'" The team at NDSS worked to get to so many individual offices in Congress by building up a coalition of Sara Wolff's grassroots army and a group of professional experts who knew the ins and outs of the legislation, the bill text, and how the legislation would affect an individual with a disability.

If you keep the long term in mind, even slow-building relationships with decision-makers can be hugely productive over time. And with movements as potentially powerful as the one behind the ABLE Act, a few extra years to make sure the act was drafted well so it would be passed into law quickly was well worth it for the tens of millions of people with disabilities.

THE FIVE STAGES OF ENGAGEMENT

WHILE AT CHANGE.ORG, I got a unique perspective into the world of decision-makers because of the more than one thousand campaigns started every day on the site asking people and institutions for change. From the data, I've seen that there are a series of predictable stages decision-makers tend to go through as they react to campaigns that are directed at them. I call them the Five Stages of Engagement: denial, listening, acceptance, embracing, and empowering. Not all decision-makers go through each of the five stages, but we do see each of these stages play out on a regular basis.

Understanding the stages can help you be more effective in persuading decision-makers that you are working to influence. In particular, helping decision-makers see the risks that come from denial and the benefits that come from listening and then acting can help you make your own case more persuasive. For the purposes of describing each stage briefly below, I've referenced petitions to corporate decision-makers, since they take place in a shorter time frame and clearly demonstrate each stage. Nevertheless, these stories illustrate the way decision-makers of all types react to appeals for change.

1. DENIAL

The first stage in this process, as with the five stages of grief, is denial. Some decision-makers would prefer to stick to business as usual and act as if nothing is changing around them. A good example here is SeaWorld—a well-regarded business that came under intense pressure after a 2013 documentary called *Blackfish* criticized the treatment of orcas held in captivity at water parks, including their properties. There was major public outcry, expressed in part through dozens of campaigns on Change.org. Although Sea-World initially tried to actively fight the criticism, even running a pro-orca SeaWorld advertising campaign, partners started to pull away and business receded dramatically as public dissent grew. Eventually, they were forced to take action. In March 2016, Sea-World decided to stop orca breeding as well as orca shows, instead redirecting its focus to educational programs.

Surprisingly, after years of denying the issue, the move turned out to be *better* for their business in the end. According to *New York* magazine, "The existential battle they had been so desperately fighting was over something that people didn't even want anymore. . . . [A] survey of 2,400 people across the country, found that . . . SeaWorld's favorability score would rise 11 to 27 points." If they had been able to move from denial faster, SeaWorld could have spared itself the huge hit to its reputation and saved tens of millions of dollars. If you can help decision-makers understand that taking action may not only protect their reputation but also be better for their business, you'll have a better chance of getting the outcome you want.

2. LISTENING

The second stage is listening, when decision-makers can't or aren't yet ready to do what is being asked of them, but want to engage and have a dialogue to show they are willing to hear feedback. Sometimes just being heard, knowing that your voice matters, and starting a dialogue can be huge steps in driving your movement forward. An initial request for just a meeting or a conversation may be a less threatening way to start a relationship with a decision-maker—and it may lead to further action.

At the end of 2014, Renee Posey, an Old Navy customer, started a campaign on Change.org. She was frustrated that Old Navy charged more for plus-size clothing for women, whereas plus-size men's clothing wasn't priced at a premium. Renee's petition gained nearly 100,000 signatures. National media including *Good Morning America* picked up the story, leading to a fair amount of backlash for Old Navy. But then the company decided to meet with Renee and listen to what she had to say. Renee wasn't a critic of Old Navy; she was a customer. And she loved the brand; she just wanted to see fair treatment between men and women. In an interview with the *Huffington Post*, Renee explained that during a conference call with three executives from Old Navy and its parent company, Gap Inc., she asked that they start thinking about a plan to address consumer concerns—namely, to eliminate the differential in plus-size clothing prices, make a larger selection of new plus-size styles available, and change their return policy so that online plus-size purchases could be exchanged in stores.

Instead of getting defensive, the executives made it clear to Renee that they understood her concerns and intended to do something about them. Though they didn't agree to all of her asks right away, they did agree to take some important immediate steps. They began accepting plus-size returns in stores and put together an advisory group of plus-size women, including Renee, to better understand that part of their customer base. While she didn't get everything she'd wanted all at once, and some of the signers of her petition were upset by that, Renee was so happy that Old Navy listened and took action that she marked the campaign a victory and wrote an update to the signers praising Old Navy and Gap Inc. for their initial steps.

If you let decision-makers know that you are open to starting with a conversation in which all parties can express their perspectives, it can serve as a starting point to prompt potential action. There may be alternative solutions to a problem that can only be discovered by listening to each other.

3. ACCEPTANCE

Stage three is acceptance: decision-makers listen to the people asking them for change, agree that what they are asking for makes sense, and then decide to do what is being asked of them. It is just "acceptance," though, because while they agree to make the change, they don't go any further to more deeply engage with their customers or constituents around it, or promote it to make it a core part of their platform or brand.

A survivor of workplace sexual assault started a petition in 2013 asking LinkedIn to create a blocking feature. She had quit her job but was stalked by her harasser on LinkedIn. She used two techniques we already know are effective: she shared her personal story to make the problem more visceral, and used data to make her case more persuasive, noting that all other major social networks already had a blocking feature, except for LinkedIn. Her campaign was effective: LinkedIn did launch a blocking feature, and Paul Rockwell, head of trust and safety at LinkedIn, posted a decision-maker response and said, "We know members have requested a blocking feature on LinkedIn. I come to you today to assure you that your concerns were heard loud and clear. We built this feature not only because it was a feature our members requested, but because we also knew it was the right thing to do." The reaction from their customers was very positive, and they got some reasonable press coverage from it as well, mainly from people happy to hear that the feature was finally available. You are in good shape if you can persuade a decision-maker to get all the way to the acceptance stage.

4. EMBRACING

The fourth stage of engagement is embracing, when decision-makers actively embrace the requests from the people who are asking them for change. They make changes that go beyond what movement leaders ask for, and potentially promote the changes that they are making in order to cultivate an even more loyal and excited set of customers or constituents. When Laura Coryton from London, England, learned in 2015 that tampons and other sanitary products were assessed an extra 5 percent value-added tax (VAT) that is typically assigned to "luxury" items such as helicopters and exotic meats like alligator, she was shocked. So she launched a campaign called #EndTamponTax, gathered 320,000 signatures, and persuaded the British government to pass a law confirming that sanitary products are essential, not luxury items, and to abolish the tax. It has since become a massive movement, spawning sister campaigns in other countries that tax sanitary products as luxury items, like France, Germany, Australia, and Malaysia.

However, although the law was passed in 2016, the actual tax will still be in effect until 2018. In mid-2017, Tesco, one of the largest supermarkets in the UK, stepped forward to engage with their customers around this issue. Instead of just waiting for the tax to go away, they decided to lower the price by 5 percent on nearly one hundred sanitary products to make up for the 5 percent tax. This was a huge win for their brand and extremely well received by their customers. Furthermore, it will likely be a financial win as customers flock to

TESCO offers to pay the tampon tax for their customers.   ALICE GRAY

Tesco for its lower prices. Laura now has an active petition asking other supermarkets and pharmacies to follow Tesco's lead.

5. EMPOWERING

The final stage of the engagement is empowering, and this is where the process flips upside down. In this final stage, decision-makers actually empower their consumers or their constituents to act on their behalf and to become advocates *in support of the causes the decision-makers care about.* In effect, the decision-maker has now become the movement starter. Some companies, like Airbnb, Lyft, and Uber, have begun to empower their customers (or potential customers) to advocate on the brands' behalf with local legislators to allow their services in various cities.

Luanne Calvert, then CMO of Virgin America and mastermind behind their viral safety video, had already helped to build the airline into a movement. She knew that Virgin had customers so passionate that they would get behind the brand if they were asked. When it came time to negotiate with the Dallas airport authority to try to get access to two gates that were becoming available at Dallas Love Field airport, Virgin America went straight to its customers. Virgin rallied its loyal supporters by starting a Change.org petition asking people to sign if they supported the idea of Virgin America getting the two gates at the Dallas airport. Virgin called the campaign "Free Love Field"—and won. With 27,000 signatures in two weeks, Virgin secured the two gates and created a huge business win and victory for its brand.

• • •

I RECENTLY SPOKE at a health-care conference attended by the heads of many large insurance companies and other major health-care stakeholders. They were concerned about how to handle the increasing amount of pressure from their own customers now that people can so easily spread messages on social media. And they were especially worried whether they would set untenable precedents by agreeing to cover previously uncovered drugs or procedures. I sympathize with the feeling of being caught between a rock and a hard place. But if they and other decision-makers could start to think of themselves as building a movement that their own customers could support—like the movements that brands from Plum Organics to Virgin have built—then they could work with their own customers to get them out of the bind. Their customers could help fight challenging regulations set by lawmakers or put pressure on drug companies to lower prices. If the people who may appear to have the least power can effectively start movements for change— survivors of crime, teenagers, the elderly, the voiceless—then shouldn't the most powerful companies be able to do the same thing?

The most effective and respected decision-makers will be the ones that move up this ladder of engagement quickly and see that there are actually economic incentives for being responsive—as well as the incentive to do what's right. Those who choose not to engage in the near term will likely be forced to in the long term as incentives change and power continues to shift toward citizens and customers. So, as a movement starter, ask decision-makers: *"Do you want to lead, or do you want to follow?"* Helping decision-makers understand the benefit of being in the vanguard of change can be one of the most effective persuasion tools.

• • •

ONCE YOU'VE MOVED through the steps necessary to achieving your vision—creating a Theory of Change, getting early supporters on board, and working effectively with decision-makers—to help your movement maintain momentum, you'll need to think about ways to get the most out of the team of people supporting your cause. The more you can motivate your supporters to take action, the more successful your movement will be.

5

LEAD YOUR CREW

Inspiring teams

Contrary to what I believed as a little girl, being the boss almost never involves marching around, waving your arms, and chanting, "I am the boss! I am the boss!"

—TINA FEY

LEADERSHIP IS LEADERSHIP IS LEADERSHIP

ONCE YOU'VE CLARIFIED your vision and built early momentum, the next big step to tackle is how to keep people motivated and inspired to be part of your fight. Whether you've found supporters from scratch by leveraging influencers and social media, or you have a built-in team because you are starting a new company or proposing a new idea within an existing organization, your movement can't continue unless the support from your team does. Without others supporting you and spreading your cause, you really don't have a movement.

The good news is that the skills required to inspire and empower people to support and grow your movement are the same whether inside a company, on a sports team, in a classroom, or within the halls of government. Some of the techniques in this chapter are typically used by people who lead more formal teams, but I believe these concepts are useful even for ad hoc teams. Movements often have one charismatic leader at the head, but they don't work to make change unless everyone involved is invested and feels trusted to carry the cause forward. That's why we need to remember one crucial thing: *a team is made up of individuals—and you build a movement by motivating every single person on your team to fight for the cause.*

I first realized this when I was a coxswain on the crew team in college. It's true for rowers, and it's true for all the teams I've been a part of since. When I was a coxswain, it was important for me to find ways to motivate the whole crew, but it was just as critical to understand how to motivate each individual rower. The way I determined what worked best with each rower was to coach each person individually on the rowing machine, trying different techniques to test what made the difference between a good time and a great time for each person. For some it was encouraging feedback, such as saying, "I know you can do this," and for others it was competitive feedback, such as, "Don't let so-and-so beat your time."

Different motivators worked for different people, and learning how to push them each in unique ways led to better results and more wins as a team. At work, I now use a tool I developed to understand the factors that drive each member of the team.

Many years ago, I was leading a team of talented marketers at Yahoo! when something unexpected happened. In a one-on-one meeting, one woman on my team said to me, "I want you to know that if I ever do a really good job, just pay me more money. I don't care about recognition or awards, and I'm not motivated by praise. If I do well, just give me a bonus or pay me more."

I stuttered through a response, feeling a bit taken aback by her comments. But as I thought about the conversation more, I realized something: if this team member hadn't told me what motivated her, I'd likely never know. What's worse, I might try to reward her for good work in a way that would be motivating for *me* but not at all for her, leaving her frustrated and less likely to perform well in the future.

I realized that if I wanted her to be happy and productive in her job, the most helpful tools I could have in order to ensure her happiness were the details of what motivated her. This is true in other relationships, too. It is often referred to as the "platinum" rule: instead of using the "golden" rule of treating other people as *you* would like to be treated, treat them as *they* would like to be treated.

So based on this illuminating conversation, I decided that the best way to keep people happy at work was to start directly asking all the people on my teams what motivated them. To do so effectively, I created a tool: the Motivational Pie Chart. I know the name is not awesome. In fact, it was once referred to by an engineer on my team as the most Dilbert-y thing he had ever seen at work. Nevertheless, it is actually useful. Whereas performance reviews let us measure how someone is performing against the objectives the organization has set for them, the Motivational Pie Chart asks how we as an organization are performing against the criteria that motivate this specific individual. Using the tool is pretty simple. You just ask people to do a three-part exercise:

- Choose categories: Write down categories for everything that motivates you at work—recognition, compensation, learning new things, a flexible schedule, etc. You can write as many or as few things as you want, and there are no preset categories. Anything that matters to you can go on your list.
- Assign weighting: Give each category a percentage weighting in order of its importance to you. The total weightings should add up to 100 percent, thus giving you a comprehensive pie chart of the things that motivate you.
- Color code satisfaction levels: Use a "red, yellow, green" color-coding system to rate how satisfied you currently are with each of the categories on the list. If you are very satisfied with your compensation, give it a green. If you are completely dis-

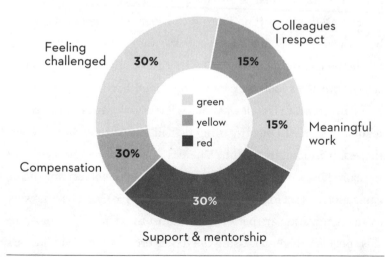

Sample Motivational Pie Chart

satisfied with how challenged you feel in your job, give that a
red, and so on.

If you are using the tool as a team leader, the next step is to have
an open conversation with each person on your team to talk about
ways you can work together to get your team member to green on
the categories they chose. Understanding what makes people happy
is a great way to make sure they stay motivated on your team and
support your movement.

Since that original conversation at Yahoo!, I've used this tool
with over a thousand people at four companies, and I've seen an
interesting pattern emerge. While there are a lot of unique factors
that can motivate individuals (I've heard everything from "I want to
be able to go rock climbing each morning" to "I'd like to be on the
cover of a magazine"), there are three key motivational factors that
most people share:

- **Purpose:** People want to do work they find meaningful so
  they know they're doing something important and deserving
  of their time and energy. And they want to understand how
  the role they play as an individual connects to the mission of
  the organization.
- **Growth:** People want to continue learning new things over
  time and feel challenged by their work. If they stop feeling
  like they are growing and developing, they lose motivation.
- **Connection:** People are motivated and inspired by working
  with other people they respect, admire, and trust. Being part

of a team of people they like and care about is an important part of enjoying their work.

These three factors are so common that I've seen them, using various naming conventions, in nearly every pie chart I've looked at over the past fifteen years. It's also true that money motivates people, especially if they feel they are being paid significantly less than they are worth. It's analogous to Maslow's hierarchy of needs: once people feel their basic financial needs are being met and that they are paid fairly for their capabilities, then they quickly move on to focusing on "higher level" motivators like meaning, collegiality, and learning. Note that the pie chart can and does change over time. That is to be expected—just as our lives and careers change, so do our motivations.

Understanding both the unique, individual motivators and these core, common motivators is necessary when building and leading a team of any kind. In the rest of this chapter, I'll take you through each of the three core themes to show how to put them to work to rally your team into passionate supporters of your movement. If you want to inspire people to support a vision, lead them well by making it clear why that vision has meaning, showing them how their role connects to that vision, demonstrating how they can learn and be challenged by being part of the team, and building a team of people who respect and support each other.

1. CHAMPION PURPOSE

AS I'VE EMPHASIZED throughout the book, meaningful purpose is the key to launching any movement. And as we saw in the pie chart, it's also one of the best ways to inspire any team. In this section, I'll cover a few examples of how leaders effectively use purpose to encourage and engage individuals and teams.

PURPOSE IS A BRIDGE BUILDER

Movements are often most effective when they unite many disparate threads and appeal to many different people. A clear sense of purpose can provide a source of unity. Özgecan Aslan, a nineteen-year-old Turkish university student, was murdered in 2015 on a minibus in Mersin, Turkey, as she resisted an attempted rape. She had been the last person left on a minibus when the driver diverted the route and drove into a nearby forest and tried to rape her. When she resisted by using pepper spray, he stabbed her several times and beat her to death with an iron rod. He then called his father and a friend to help him dispose of the body. They burned her body and cut off Özgecan's hands to try to destroy evidence in the case.

When Gözde Salur, a young Turkish woman, heard about Özgecan, she couldn't help but feel that such a crime could easily have happened to her. Gözde was also a university student at the time, and she commuted to and from school on the same kind of minibus that Özgecan's attacker drove. The news scared her, and though she had never been involved in political activism, her sense of connection to a woman she had never met and frustration about a culture that tolerated this kind of violence against women spurred her to act. She said that "crimes against women are a part of our everyday lives. But the brutal murder of Özgecan was a last straw. My conscience, my heart, could not handle hearing that one more suspect had been let off in court just because he wore a nice suit." That was the moment she realized she wanted to take action.

Gözde started a petition to pass "Özgecan's Law" to prevent reduced sentences for those convicted of violence against women based on "good behavior" or "unjust provocation." Soon, despite how fractured her country was politically, she saw that people were coming together around her campaign to mobilize for justice after this brutal crime. A sense of shared purpose had created a community of people united in this one goal, even if they were divided in others. When the signatures on her petition started to increase, she said to me, "It showed me that regardless of political views, social position, and everything else, people can still come together in Turkey to raise their voices in support of such an important issue. I received messages from very, very different people through Change.org and through Facebook and my Twitter account. These people had very different political views. Some of them were conservatives, some of them were very liberal. But they all told me, 'We are with you. If there's anything we can do, please let us know.' And this showed me that we could connect in such moments. This gave me a lot of hope that there's still many things that this society can do when we come together."

Gözde's work paid off: 1.2 million people signed the petition.

Those 1.2 million people made hers the most-signed Change.org campaign of all time in Turkey. And while the law has not yet passed due to the ongoing political upheaval resulting from the attempted 2016 military coup, Parliament is considering a draft proposal for the law. Furthermore, the three men convicted in the murder of Özgecan were all given life sentences, showing a marked shift in the treatment of men who commit crimes against women. People from a wide variety of perspectives and backgrounds united around Gözde's vision for Özgecan's Law and became part of the movement to create harsher penalties for perpetrators of violence against women.

EXPOSE YOUR TEAM TO STORIES OF PURPOSE

Within existing organizations, leaders are also more effective when they keep the organization's purpose at the forefront. One of the best ways to do that is by making the stories of people who are affected by your vision front and center. Neil Grimmer of Plum Organics, whom we met in Chapter 1, reminded his team of his vision in a weekly all-hands meeting they held on Monday mornings. Each meeting would end with a section called "The Love Bomb," which showed a picture and a story from one of their consumers about how Plum had made a difference in that family's life. Neil calls this catalyzing tool one of the most powerful things they could have done as a company because it helped them start the week realizing that what they do is important. He says, "Even when the work you do matters, you can still feel like sometimes you're just punching in and punching out. But that reminder, when it's front and center the first thing Monday morning, gives you that rocket fuel to get past that moment."

We used a similar process to keep people close to the mission at Change.org. In weekly all-team video calls including colleagues from across the globe, we would often share a video from a petition starter or even have one join the team on the call and talk about how the platform made a difference in his or her life. These stories were almost always very emotional, as the people using the site were usually overcoming major personal challenges. The ability to directly connect people on the team to people using the platform was an extremely powerful tool in ensuring the team felt close to the purpose of the organization and was especially effective for team members whose roles were a bit more distant from the day-to-day purpose, like those with roles in finance, engineering, and other departments.

The organizations that are most effective in reinforcing purpose among their teams find ways to either share stories or make connections between people who use the products and the people who build and support them. There are many ways to do that. You can have a smaller, more frequent meetings like Plum and Change.org do; you can have bigger, less frequent, but more intense events that bring people together, like eBay Live, a conference that brought together buyers, sellers, and eBay staff; or you can do both. My team at Facebook, for example, uses a two-pronged strategy. We regularly bring in different Facebook group administrators to meet with the team and hold big events like Community Summits, where Facebook employees meet and interact with administrators for hundreds of the largest groups. Big events like this can help cement community, not only between your team and the people who use your product or support your cause, but also among the supporters. Even informal meetings can bring critical learning to your team about how to pursue your cause or product in a way that will best meet the needs of the people whose lives you aim to improve. The better you and your team understand the people you hope to have an impact on, the more likely you will be to meet their needs, and the more closely you'll all feel connected to your purpose.

EXTEND YOUR PURPOSE TO OTHERS

Neil Grimmer talks a lot about how values-driven businesses will be at the center of the new economy, specifically because of how motivating that core purpose is for the people who work there. And he hopes to prove this again in his new business, Habit, which offers personalized health testing and nutrition planning to people looking to have a healthier lifestyle. Echoing Plum's origin story, Neil started Habit when no other companies existed to meet his personal needs. Although he had been a triathlete in his earlier days, Neil told me that after eight years of running Plum, he had succumbed to what his doctor called "CEO coping mechanisms"—too much bad food, booze, and coffee, and not enough sleep. He had gained fifty pounds, and after finally going to see doctors he found out he was prediabetic and had a high risk of heart attack.

Instead of just stopping with the doctor visits, Neil started biohacking and meeting with amazing scientists around the country and around the world; he even had his DNA tested through whole genome sequencing. Through this process he gathered an enormous amount of insight into what was going on with his body. Neil realized that what he was going through was not unique to him and that his personal discovery could be valuable to others. As he told me, "I realized that the insights I was getting about myself, through thousands of dollars and some world travel to visit different specialists, needed to be accessible to everybody at affordable price points, democratized in a way that empowered people to take control of their lives through food."

So Neil is now building a second business based on a personal experience that made him deeply feel the importance of the connection between health and food. While others on his team (or people he had yet to recruit to join his team) may not have originally shared his purpose, the depth of Neil's passion helped him attract, hire, and inspire incredible talent for the Habit team, from their chief scientist to their chief technology officer. Neil's clear purpose was also central in recruiting experts to Habit's advisory board, like Dr. Leroy Hood, who is one of the founders of the Human Genome Project. A clear purpose can help you not only to keep a team inspired but also to build an amazing team in the first place.

TRACK YOUR PROGRESS

In order to know whether you're making a difference, you need to track your progress. Often, people track core metrics that have to do with business success, like revenue and audience growth, but neglect to track the metrics that actually correspond to their vision and Theory of Change. Admittedly, it's not always easy to find metrics that align perfectly when it's likely that the vision you are aiming to achieve is something that hasn't been done before. But even though measuring impact isn't as neat and clean as simply measuring revenue or daily active users, it is critical to inspiring your team. We know that people are motivated by meaning in their work, and being able to measure it helps people see just how much their work matters. Wharton professor and bestselling author Adam Grant showed the connection between meaningful work, motivation, and results in a study he conducted with the University of Michigan's fund-raising call center. When callers were able to speak to a student who had benefited from their fund-raising efforts and hear the student's gratitude for the scholarship, the results were striking: within a month, the callers increased the length of their phone calls with potential donors by 142 percent—and increased the amount of donations they solicited by 171 percent. A later study showed continued increases in revenues—by more than 400 percent.

At Change.org, where the vision is a world where no one is powerless, measuring impact meant trying to understand how to measure people's sense of their own agency. We started by trying to use pure quantitative metrics, looking specifically at the metrics for petition victories. Initially, we concentrated on the number of people experiencing victories, assuming that if someone had been part of a campaign that won, then it likely meant that they would feel more empowered and have a stronger sense that change was possible. That metric grew from 8 million people to nearly 100 million people over a five-year period. While that was terrific on its own merits, we realized that we didn't have a real sense of whether this truly changed the way people felt about their own power. Ultimately, we created something called the "empowerment index," which uses qualitative metrics from surveys. Combined with the victory metrics, the company can get a good sense of whether it's making progress toward its vision. And that, in turn, helps the team believe in the impact they are creating and see meaning in their work.

2. CULTIVATE GROWTH

THOUGH IT MAY be counterintuitive, one of the most effective ways to keep individuals and teams motivated is to continually challenge them. People feel more excited to work hard as part of a team and in support of a cause when they feel they are learning and growing as part of the process. This section will cover some examples of how effective leaders can cultivate growth among the people on their teams.

THE POWER OF HIGH EXPECTATIONS

Research has demonstrated for years that high expectations have the power to improve performance. Experts call this phenomenon the Pygmalion Effect. Named after a sculptor in a Greek myth who fell in love with a statue he carved, the Pygmalion Effect occurs when an authority figure's positive expectations lead to the improved performance of another person.

The effect was first demonstrated in 1966 by Harvard researcher Robert Rosenthal. He told teachers which of their students (about 20 percent) would be intellectual "bloomers," saying those students' results on a test suggested they would have surprising gains in IQ over the next eight months. The teachers were not told that the students on that list were actually selected at random. Eight months later, they retested the IQs of the randomly selected students and found they had improved, especially as compared to a control group. The teachers' high expectations of the students they were told were intellectual bloomers caused the teachers to change their own interactions with those students such that the students had more belief in themselves and their ability to improve, and therefore actually did improve. The effect has been demonstrated many times since then with people in a wide variety of situations, ranging from military recruits to corporate sales teams.

In 2015, Jack Zenger and Joseph Folkman, who run a leadership consultancy, looked at the performance and engagement of people who worked for managers who gave more high ratings on performance reviews to their teams versus those who consistently gave lower ratings. Even though both sets of managers felt they were setting high expectations for their teams, their teams' results diverged dramatically. As Zenger and Folkman describe in *Harvard Business Review*, "The people who'd received more positive ratings felt lifted up and supported. And that vote of confidence made them more optimistic about future improvement. Conversely, subordinates rated by the consistently tougher managers were confused or discouraged— often both. They felt they were not valued or trusted, and that it was impossible to succeed." The actual belief that leaders had in the people on their team became a self-fulfilling prophecy, leading the people who felt their managers believed in them to *actually* improve. This is not to suggest that managers should artificially inflate ratings for people on their teams but rather that managers who have confidence in their teams tend to build higher-performing teams.

● ● ●

WHEN YOU SET high expectations for people and then believe in them and support them to reach those expectations, they can soar far beyond what you (and even they) expect. And not only do people perform better when they feel trusted and supported, they also respect and trust their leaders more, too. I've seen this as a coxswain and at every company where I've worked, but the most profound example in my experience was when I was a schoolteacher myself, early in my career.

When I was in college, I taught during the summers in a program called Summerbridge, now part of a national collaborative called Breakthrough, which helps highly motivated, low-income middle school students get on the path to college. At Breakthrough, all of the teachers are high school or college students themselves. Nevertheless, they're given full responsibility for curriculum development, classroom teaching, and mentorship to the amazing young people in the program. I was only seventeen when I started teaching there, and to be entrusted with so much responsibility at such a young age was incredibly empowering. Wanting to deserve that trust made me work even harder, so I threw everything I had into being the best teacher and mentor I could be, and to learning as much as I could from the people around me.

Most of the students in this program were going to be the first in their families to go to college, and they didn't always have an easy road to get there. Many of them lived in areas rife with gang violence; often, they were being raised by grandparents or single parents, or by parents who didn't speak English. Many had to care for younger siblings at home or work to support their families. Despite all that, or perhaps because of it, they were *incredibly* motivated— motivated enough to fill out a long and very challenging application with essays and teacher recommendations, which, if they were successful and accepted to the program, would require them to spend their entire summer in school. Instead of thinking about relaxing, they were preparing for six weeks of full-day classes, followed by two hours of homework each night.

And they were *excited* about it.

It was the first environment they had been a part of where it was cool to be smart, where they could bond with other kids who loved learning, and where they could connect with role models who were just a few years ahead of them, showing them that the journey they wanted to take was possible.

The magic of Breakthrough is the opportunity for true empowerment: the organization and the leadership set high expectations for both the students and the teachers in terms of the outcomes they believe can be achieved. And because those high expectations are made clear and the support to reach them is there, people feel trusted and almost always reach or exceed them. This is true for the Breakthrough middle school students, over 90 percent of whom go on to graduate from four-year colleges. And it is true of the student teachers, more than 70 percent of whom go on to careers in education. It was also true for me. I went on to teach high school and to found my own Breakthrough program in Pittsburgh, which is still running twenty-five years later and has helped thousands of young people become first-generation college graduates. Many of those students came back to teach in the program, and one—Sarah Bachner—even became the director of the program for several years. This is another reason why movements are so powerful—when strong enough, they can continue even after the original leader departs. Other people from within the movement will pick up the torch and keep running.

Breakthrough, started by the incredible Lois Loofbourrow in San Francisco, is now a national collaborative with twenty-four affiliate sites around the United States and one in Hong Kong. All together, Breakthrough has prepared many tens of thousands of first-generation college students over the past several decades. It is precisely this belief in the potential of people and the setting of high expectations for them that causes people to be so passionate about Breakthrough in return.

90/10 DECISION-MAKING

One way to institutionalize high expectations and help people grow is what I call the 90/10 model for decision-making, something I've used at Change.org as well as other places I've worked. The core idea is that people should be able to make roughly 90 percent of the decisions that are required for them to get their job done. The remaining 10 percent of decisions may require sign-off or approval. If this isn't happening, either you're asking people to do things that you shouldn't be asking them to do, or you're not empowering them as much as you should be.

One way Change.org implemented the 90/10 model is through a "traffic light" system. Here's how it works:

- 90 percent of any given person's decisions should be green— they can make those decisions on their own, without needing to check with anyone or get approval. (Note: People can still ask for input or even guidance on these "green" decisions; they just don't require someone else's approval.)
- 5 percent of decisions are red—when the person knows they will definitely need to get the approval of a manager or senior leader. These are usually decisions that are hard to reverse, affect other areas of the organization, or involve large budgets.
- The remaining 5 percent of decisions are yellow—when people are not sure whether it is an approval-requiring red or a go-ahead green, at which point they should double-check with their manager to find out.

Creating structural clarity like this helps to ensure that (a) people get to make enough of their own decisions to feel trusted and empowered, and (b) people have a common language for discussing decision-making in a clear, nonthreatening way.

To see whether you are on track for the 90/10 system, you can use a log to track decision-making. Typically, a decision log tracks which decisions were made, by whom, on which dates, the primary rationale, and who was consulted. A decision log can help in two ways: First, it shows you whether people on your team are actually able to make most of their decisions on their own. If it turns out that's not the case, the log provides a good starting point for open discussions between leaders and people on their teams. Focus on determining where the decision-making process breaks down and how you can establish clearer expectations about who makes which decisions. Second, it provides visibility for people on the team who weren't involved in the decision. In leadership-level meetings at Google, we would track all of our major decisions and distribute the log to our full teams following the meeting. It created complete transparency about what decisions were made, by whom, and why.

GROWTH THROUGH DIVERSITY

As you build your team, don't forget that the highest performing teams are diverse ones made up of people with different skills, different backgrounds and experiences, and different demographic traits such as gender, race, age, socioeconomic status, and sexual orientation.

There is an enormous amount of research on this topic from studies spanning several decades showing that diverse teams are more innovative and lead to better financial results, higher growth rates, and even higher quality scientific research results. People who think differently and bring diverse perspectives to the table challenge us to get outside our comfort zone, consider different questions, and push our ideas further. So when you think about how to inspire a team, remember that getting help from people who think differently than you do is extremely valuable. It's especially helpful as a tool for growth and development because people continually learn when they're part of teams with a diversity of perspectives to push their thinking.

The person who has taught me the most about this is my husband, Len. He comes from a large German and Polish Catholic family—eight brothers and sisters—and grew up in a modest house in a blue-collar neighborhood in Pittsburgh. Neither of his parents went to college, and Len was able to put himself through college by joining the military. He spent twenty years in the military in a combination of active duty and the National Guard. (He actually flew home on a one-day pass for our wedding.) So much of what I loved about Len when we first met and what I love about him now comes from the experiences that shaped him. He is hardworking, a creative and scrappy problem-solver, always willing to lend a hand to someone else, and kind at his core. I sometimes joke that I married him because whenever we went to someone's house for dinner, he was always the first person to get up and help with the dishes.

I come from a small, upper-middle-class Jewish family and grew up in San Francisco. While my parents came from humble backgrounds as the children of Eastern European Jewish immigrants, they were both able to go to college, get master's degrees, and become executives in their professions. And though I worked paying jobs from the age of fourteen, I did not have to work to pay my way through college, and I grew up with other privileges that shaped my worldview, like the ability to travel internationally.

Having the combined perspectives of our families is so valuable to both of us and to our daughters. We're able to appreciate and learn from different religions, different class backgrounds, and generally different perspectives on the world. My daughters have also seen that although we are different, there is more that ties us together than pulls us apart. Understanding that we have so much in common despite the differences in our backgrounds *and* that we have so much to learn from each other also makes it easier to remain open-minded to the idea that *anyone* might have something to teach us. In fact, the more different we are, the more likely we have something to learn.

Learning from those who are different from me has been one of the things I've enjoyed most about my various jobs as well, even when it can be difficult sometimes to find common ground. My co-founder and I at The Dealmap came from quite different backgrounds and perspectives, and it was the first time running a startup company for both of us, which was a fairly stressful experience. The biggest area of contention between us was our different decision-making styles. He had spent his early years at Microsoft, which has a much more hierarchical, top-down decision-making structure, and I was used to a more input-gathering-based decision-making model. He really wanted me to just decide things, and I wanted to make sure I heard ideas from the other leaders on the team before making a final decision. We spent most of our first year working through how to work together—and it sometimes got so heated that we'd have to go outside or into a car to have discussions so we wouldn't upset the team. But after many months of working through our different styles, we began to appreciate each other more, learn from one another, and we both came out stronger for it. We were able to build The Dealmap into a successful company together—more successfully than either of us could have done alone—we grew in our effectiveness as leaders, and we remain dear friends today.

At a time when our world seems more divided than ever, it's also more important than ever to reach out to people with alternate views and experiences. When you look to inspire others, remember you can't do it alone, or at least that you can't do it *as well* alone as you can with the help of those who bring something to the table that you don't.

SEEK ADVICE

In 2013 two amazing women on the team at Change.org—Sarah Ryan and Michelle Melendez—along with a few others helped to found Women Helping Others Achieve (WHOA), an employee-led peer-mentoring program to build leadership skills and provide a support network for women at all levels of the company. Though they came from very different backgrounds and worked in different departments at our global company, they both felt something was needed to help women succeed at work and in their lives outside of it and decided to try to create a new program to solve that problem.

After discussing it among a small group and getting executive buy-in, Michelle and Sarah decided that the key next step was to get more input from people across the company who would be involved.

As Sarah described to me in an interview: "We knew that we had the passion and the enthusiasm and the support from the executive staff. The next step was getting more buy-in, and more diverse input. We gathered together women from every region, from every department, and we made sure that we had a breadth of experience levels in there, too. We knew that we needed this diversity of thought and experience to make sure that the program was helpful and supportive for all women at Change and not just a subset of women in a certain office or department. So we had that take-off call, and it was really exciting. Everybody had lots of great ideas." And many of those great ideas became critical pieces of the program.

Michelle and Sarah saw a need they wanted to address inside their organization, both for themselves and for others. Although they didn't have all the answers, they took the leap to get started and pulled in others to push the idea further. By asking for advice, they not only made the program stronger, but they also grew as leaders and gave the rest of the team opportunities to grow as well. And, as an added benefit, engaging their participants deepened the connections that they felt with the program, and with Michelle and Sarah as leaders. It was a successful approach. Three years later, WHOA was thriving within Change.org, with nearly every woman participating, and it had expanded beyond the co-mentorship program to a speaker series, a chat room with shared experiences, and more.

While asking others for advice is a great strategy to promote growth and learning, it is also an effective way to improve people's impression of your competence and likability as a leader. Research by Alison Wood Brooks and Francesca Gino of Harvard Business

School showed in multiple studies that when people ask for advice, they are seen as smarter and more likable by those they ask, primarily because people like to be asked for advice—it makes them in turn feel smart and appreciated. This held true in a wide variety of situations across studies by different people, from job interviews to performance reviews and even to speed dating! Being willing to ask for advice will not only help you and your team grow, it will also likely make people view you as a stronger leader.

IMAGINE THE HORIZON

In the same way that you have a long-term vision for your movement, helping your team create a long-term vision is one way to keep them motivated and to encourage their growth as well.

There's a technique called the Horizon Conversation that I use with my team and that I adapted from David Hanrahan, former head of HR at Change.org. Similar to the Theory of Change that we talked about in Chapter 3, it's a way of starting with the outcome that you want and then working backward to figure how to get there.

The Horizon Conversation has three parts.

The first is an assessment of the skills you've already learned, based on the roles you've had so far in your life. The initial step is to go back through your life and say, "These are all of my experiences," and then pull out the top few lessons you believe you learned in each of those roles. That adds up to your current set of skills.

The second part is to think about a goal you want to set: "What do I want to be doing five to ten years from now?" The objective here is to think big and not limit yourself to options that are obvious or in a "straight line" to what you are doing now. I've done this activity with many people and heard goals that vary from starting a business, to going into politics, to becoming an author or an artist, to being a CEO, to wanting to start movements of their own. There are no limits to people's dreams. I never rein in people's goals, because that's the point of the exercise: to look ahead to the vast horizon and dream about what's possible. Once you have your dreams outlined, make a list of all the skills that are needed for that role you want. If you aren't sure, you can work with someone who understands that specific role to make a list of the skills required to be great at it.

The third step is to look at the gaps between the skills you have now and those required for where you want to be so you understand what it's going to take to get there. And then you can think about specific roles and projects you can take on between here and there to make sure you're on the path that is heading to the horizon, to where you want to be.

It may seem crazy to put huge, seemingly unachievable goals on the table, but the truth is, the best chance people have of reaching enormous goals is to be specific about what those goals are and how to work toward them. As with your vision for your movement overall, the only way to actually achieve a goal is to be clear about what you want and go all in on getting there. And the same holds true for your team. If you want them to be able to truly grow and achieve big dreams, then it makes sense to help them outline those dreams and take steps toward getting there.

YOU CAN TAKE ONLY SO MANY POWER 10S

Motivation of teams and individuals is as much an art as it is a science—and it is crucial to know the fine line between inspiring people to give their all in a positive way and pushing them too hard toward burnout. There is a technique in rowing called a "Power 10," when rowers in a boat will take ten strokes at their absolute maximum power. They are already rowing at an intense pace, and these ten strokes are meant to lift that intensity even higher, usually to try to move past another boat in a race when it's really close.

The coxswain decides when to call these Power 10s and how many to call during a given race. What I found, after coxing for years, is that a team can usually take only two or three Power 10s in one race—too many and they stop being effective because the team gets too tired, too few and another team may overtake you with its own Power 10.

The concept of the Power 10 applies to other forms of leading teams as well. The cliché that "life is a marathon and not a sprint" certainly resonates, but what it leaves out is that having some sprints can make us more likely to reach our goals. When we are focused on rallying a team around a vision and on ensuring that the team feels they are being sufficiently challenged, then a few well-placed Power 10s can work miracles. Having a deadline that requires an all-nighter, working together to persuade a particularly hard-to-move decision-maker, or brainstorming to overcome a technical obstacle are all Power 10s that can serve to bring a team together. The key is to use these sprints sparingly, and then to really go all in when you need to. Selectively leveraging "all in" moments will help ensure the team feels like they are being challenged without being pushed too far.

3. FOSTER CONNECTIONS

AFTER MEANINGFUL PURPOSE and a clear path for growth, the third critical area of focus is to build strong, trusting connections, both between yourself and your team and among members of the team. Recent data from a two-year study of effective teams at Google showed that one of the top factors in high performing teams is psychological safety: Do members of the team feel safe to take risks and be vulnerable in front of each other? In this section we'll cover techniques and examples of how leaders build trust between team members, resulting in the psychological safety that helps teams operate at their best.

BASK IN RELATIONSHIPS

In the same way that my mom taught me about grit and determination, everything I learned about making connections with people I picked up from my dad. My father immerses himself in relationships with people; he loves learning about them, about their families, their interests, and their backgrounds. And then he remembers—he remembers everything people tell him, making them feel understood and appreciated and etching deep relationships with people over time. (His incredible memory is also the reason he is the king of Trivial Pursuit and knows the words to every song.) He does this over years and years, so now he has meaningful relationships with people from all stages of his life and in many parts of the world.

And he is a storyteller. By combining his amazing memory about what makes someone unique with his gift of storytelling, my dad is able to expertly weave people together like yarn, making connections between new people who don't yet know each other, and who often end up to be great friends. These skills have not only helped him be more successful in his career through an increasingly large and well-connected network, but also (and perhaps more important), these relationships have given him a lifetime of joy.

These are valuable skills to have when aiming to build connections with your team. Creating an authentic relationship with someone begins by understanding who they are and what they care about. If you start by approaching people with openness and a genuine desire to learn about them, you are much more likely to build lasting relationships that tie you and your team closer together.

THE POWER OF COMMUNITY

In my role at Facebook, I get to see every day how individuals can bring together groups of people with shared identity and purpose into passionate communities around topics as diverse as parenting, shared health conditions, religion, race, politics, professions, and an enormous range of shared interests, from birding to motorcycles, and from science memes to musicals. Sometimes these communities grow over years, adding new members as they learn about the group from other members or friends, and sometimes they explode overnight, like Jennifer Cardenas's group for Hurricane Harvey and other groups created to help people after natural disasters.

One thing that all the successful communities have in common is one or a small number of group administrators who serve as "hosts" for the communities. They welcome people to the group when they join, they set the tone and culture, they monitor and remove bad behavior when it happens, and they add new content and ideas to the group, especially early on. Caterina Fake, the founder of Flickr, told me that starting a community is like hosting a cocktail party. When people arrive, you need to take their coats, offer them drinks, introduce them to a few people—make them feel comfortable (and step in if someone else insults them). If this early hosting is done well, then the community begins to blossom on its own, with many more members taking on the same types of activities that the initial founders did—adding content, welcoming members, setting the tone. And once many people are participating, these communities really begin to thrive.

While some communities begin with mobilization in mind, such as the disaster rescue groups or those that are set up to achieve certain goals like "Clean Up Miami Beach" or "Save Our Black Taxis" in London, others form as safe spaces for people who share interests, challenges, or ideas to connect and communicate. The thing is, even those groups—the ones not intended to drive change—have the power to mobilize their members if and when they decide that they want to. Communities where people feel safe and connected are an incredible tool to build supporters for a movement, even if you aren't sure what initial actions that movement should take. The community itself can often contribute ideas and suggestions for a plan of action. So whether you already have a clear vision, purpose, and plan, or if your purpose is clear but you aren't sure of which steps to take, building a physical or online community of people who share the same purpose is a powerful approach—and a strong foundation for change in the future.

RESPECT IS EARNED

There is a reason why rowing is frequently used as a metaphor in business, and why motivational posters often depict images of rowing (and why I've already borrowed rowing metaphors so many times). These images capture the essence of teamwork: a group of people coming together in perfect synchronicity, pushing themselves toward victory. As a coxswain, I learned incredible lessons about how to make that teamwork happen.

One of the first key lessons in coxing is that respect is earned. Coxswains need to be able to motivate a crew to push themselves beyond the limits they think they can reach, during times when they are already in pain. And they need to give constructive feedback to individual rowers in the moment, in front of their peers, or risk losing the race (a powerful lesson about the value of real-time feedback). All of this requires having the trust and respect of your team, and it doesn't come automatically just because you have a microphone.

To earn the team's respect and to build trusting connections with them, I needed to prove I was willing to work hard, too—to get in the trenches with them and feel their pain. Nearly every workout we did out of the boat, I did with them. Every hard run up sand dunes, every set climbing the stairs in the stadium, and every ice-cold run in snowy Ithaca I did alongside my team. I also listened to any feedback they had for me about how I could be more helpful as a coxswain. I worked to earn their respect and build connections with them in those moments, and then when we were in the boat, they trusted me to have their best interests in mind, to understand how they were feeling and to give reasonable feedback to them.

This principle still holds true today. When I ask my team to work late trying to reach an important goal or ship a product on time, I make sure I'm there with them—in the office or online—making it clear we're in this together. And I listen openly to any feedback they have about how I can be more effective. When you ask people to join you to support your movement—whether launching a new product or fighting for a new law—whatever your cause, if you want to inspire people, make sure that you are in it together, working as hard or harder than others you ask to help.

VULNERABILITY = POWER

We often define toughness as one of the most necessary traits for energizing a movement. But it can actually be moments of vulnerability and openness that spark the greatest change, especially when vulnerability serves to build tighter connections between a leader and his or her team. It may seem counterintuitive to suggest that laying bare your most personal struggles can make a stronger impact and help rally others behind you, but it's one of the most surprising things I learned while working at Change.org and something I saw again and again with people who start petitions. It's an idea championed by experts like Brené Brown, the University of Houston research professor and bestselling author. Not only does vulnerability make us braver in taking on the world in new ways, it also makes others want to help us do it.

Many of the most memorable movements have a profound emotional story at their core, as we've seen. One in particular epitomizes this lesson for me. John Feal was not an activist; he was a carpenter and a demolition specialist from Long Island, New York. He was a 9/11 responder, and while at the site on September 17, a piece of steel crushed his left foot. He twice applied for compensation from the September 11th Relief Fund, and was denied—even though his injury had been deemed "life-threatening and catastrophic." Because it occurred ninety-six hours after the initial event, he didn't qualify for assistance.

The experience made John realize that he was vulnerable—and so were other injured 9/11 responders. "When I got hurt on September 17, that was, at the time, the worst day of my life. Little did I know it'd probably be the most important day of my life," he told me. "My injury was gruesome and horrific. And I know now that it pales in comparison to those who are deathly ill or who have passed away. I am so minute and so small compared to these men and women in uniform and non-uniform that are dying every day or every week from 9/11-related illnesses."

For the past fifteen years, John has been working tirelessly for health benefits for 9/11 responders who suffered devastating injuries and illnesses in the aftermath of the cleanup work they did at Ground Zero. He successfully fought for the Walsh amendment that reclaimed $125 million for health issues for 9/11 responders, he started the FealGood Foundation in 2005 to further help with medical-related issues and grassroots change, and in 2015 he started a petition on Change.org to get Congress to permanently extend the health benefits covered in the Zadroga Act (which was named after James Zadroga, a New York City Police Department officer who died from illnesses attributed to the rescue and recovery work he did at ground zero).

John described what it was like to recognize his own vulnerability and why that made him even more intent on helping others: "I had to learn that I wasn't Bo Jackson, I wasn't John Wayne, and that I was a human, because in my mind I was the world's greatest athlete and I had to eat a lot of humble pie to realize that I'm fallible and I can get hurt and I can lose half a body part and I can bleed."

Acknowledging his own vulnerability also made John more effective as a leader of the movement to fight for health benefits for 9/11 responders. When John admitted his own need for help, others felt they could, too. And sharing their personal stories made even more people want to rally behind them. As John told me, "I became known as that guy that can help people. When somebody had a workman's comp hearing or Social Security hearing, I went to the hearings with them. We had to tell our personal stories, which opened up a lot of old wounds." But their willingness to tell their stories worked, both to pass the original Zadroga Act and its extension. While John may have started out as an unlikely advocate, he eventually grew into the role. "I'm flawed. I have half a foot. I have a bad knee. I have a bad back. I have post-traumatic stress disorder. I have one kidney. If somebody who is physically and mentally flawed can stop Congress in their tracks, then just imagine what somebody with a higher IQ and who is physically gifted could do. People in the 9/11 community and people outside of the 9/11 community saw the passion and the fire in my eyes and the determination. What I bring to the table is not to accept no for an answer when we're talking about human life."

John Feal took one of the most challenging moments of his life and turned it into a fight for the advocacy of others. He's incredibly modest about his own accomplishments, and he demonstrates so clearly that a willingness to share your vulnerability can be the most powerful tool in making people feel connected to you and your cause.

EVERYBODY'S GOT SOMETHING

PART OF INSPIRING a team is letting them know that you care not only about the vision you are working to achieve but also about the people you are working with. And showing you care means demonstrating you understand that no matter how dedicated people are to the movement you are building, they also have lives, families, and commitments outside of it.

I gave a speech in London in 2015 about how our work and lives are intertwined and impossible to separate, and how that is changing the future of work. To illustrate my point, I had planned a series of questions in which I was going to ask the audience to stand up if any one of a series of incidents had ever happened to them, showing how work and life are inextricably interrelated. I thought that by the time I had asked four or five questions, maybe most of the audience would be standing and my point would become clear.

I started by asking the audience this question: "How many of you have ever received a phone call with serious medical news about yourself or a close family member at work?"

Nearly the entire audience stood up.

Even I was stunned.

It was an intense and powerful moment. People looked around and realized that we all have more in common than we think and that we are all vulnerable and human. Each of us had the memories of those moments rushing back to us, and suddenly it seemed to make sense to have more empathy for each other: you never know what someone else might be going through on what seems like any other average day to you.

One of my favorite books is *Everybody's Got Something*, by *Good Morning America* co-anchor Robin Roberts. It is a memoir about her life, and in particular about her experience surviving both breast cancer and then a rare type of blood cancer, and is all about this humbling idea of perspective. As she writes in the introduction: "In Mississippi, where I'm from, there's an understanding that hard times do not discriminate. My mother used to say, 'Everybody's got something.'" As she told NPR's *Weekend Edition Sunday*: "I remember . . . when I was unfortunately diagnosed with breast cancer in 2007 and I had that moment of—wow. You know, I can't believe I'm going through this. Why is this happening to me? And my mother sweetly—I mean, sweetly and gently said, honey, everybody's got something. And it just really stuck with me. . . . It's like . . . my something is no bigger, no more important, no anything more than anybody else."

Remembering that the people we work with may be dealing with major challenges at any given moment can make us more compassionate leaders and can help earn trust from our teams. If we can build the kind of teams where people feel comfortable sharing what is happening in their lives outside of work, then people will be more likely to commit to the company or the cause because they will feel fully supported. I've had people on my team who have dealt with the death of a parent or spouse, divorce, addiction, children with mental illness and at risk of suicide, and many more of life's biggest challenges. And when we've been able to let people know that we are there for them through those moments and everything else, it truly creates a bond that is unbreakable.

* * *

THIS LESSON HITS close to home for me, too, because I've had one of those unimaginable moments that happened at work, when I was so dependent on the people around me to carry me through. I want to be honest: I have been dreading writing this section of the book.

My own "everybody's got something" moment was the worst day of my life so far, and writing about it rehashes so many difficult emotions that I almost didn't do it. But I think it's important to acknowledge that we all have times like these. We all go through things we just aren't sure we can survive, and yet we do. I know that there are so many people who have endured stories so much worse than this, and that if sharing mine could be helpful to anyone else, then I needed to do it.

This story starts on a beautiful spring day, and I was at a winery in the Santa Cruz Mountains with my team from Yahoo! for a team-building meeting off-site. Late in the afternoon I got a phone call from my husband that our daughter Emma had had an accident at the playground. She was knocked over by another child running who hadn't seen her, and she fell hard, hitting the back of her head on cement.

The school hadn't called an ambulance after the incident. Instead, knowing that Len would arrive soon anyway, they'd waited. When he arrived to pick her up, the teachers said that she just wouldn't stop crying and that they knew something was wrong. When Len arrived and saw her condition, he knew it was bad. He called me to say that he was taking her to urgent care. He put her on the phone with me and I heard her moan; she was not responsive to my questions. I knew then, too, that it was bad. I remember instantly feeling sick to my stomach—a feeling that would only get worse when Len told me, minutes later, that when they'd arrived at the urgent care office, the doctors there had called 911 right away and that he and Emma were in an ambulance on the way to the ER.

Emma was seven years old. In first grade.

I could barely breathe.

And I was an hour away, at a winery in the mountains. Nothing could feel less important at that moment, and I was desperate to get to the hospital. We had all carpooled to the event together and I didn't have a car, but I was able to get a ride down the mountain with a generous woman on my team, Paulien Strijland, who drove me straight to the ER. I was so grateful for her.

When I got to the ER and rushed in to find Emma, the first thing I saw was Len's face, which was so pale that it was almost green. Emma was in a CAT scan machine so they could examine her brain, and at the moment I walked in she was having a seizure—essentially unconscious as her whole body shook violently. Len and I were terrified as we stood by, completely unable to help our precious daughter. The medical team rushed Emma out of the CAT scan machine and into a surgical room, telling us they would need to intubate her and put her in an induced coma while they monitored her to see if they would need to drill a hole in her skull to let out the pressure that was building from swelling and potential bleeding in her brain. I was so overwhelmed that I could barely stand up, and they brought in a chair for me. And I felt horrible, both terrified for what might happen to Emma and angry at myself that I wasn't stronger in that moment.

Days of waiting followed as we remained at her side in the intensive care unit, worried that we might lose her. Ultimately the doctors were able to bring her out of the coma when the swelling subsided. That brought an enormous wave of relief. And then came a new set of questions and fears about whether there would be any permanent brain damage from the accident.

I sat by her bedside while she remained in intensive care for the next week, and I vividly remember how each time I saw she was able to do something again for the first time, it gave me more and more of a sense of relief that she would be okay. She stayed out of school for several more weeks, and on seizure medication for several more months, but thankfully she made a full recovery, returning to school just in time for her starring role in her first-grade musical, *The Princess and the Penguin*. I don't think I've ever been so joyful as the day we watched her perform in that show.

And while those were absolutely the worst days of my life, it has put every moment since then in incredibly sharp perspective because I remember so vividly what it is like when your whole world changes in an instant and you realize just how precious the important things are.

When I think back on that time, I also realize that we're stronger than we think we are. But I also know from these experiences that the fortresses we have around us—the sense of safety and security—can fall at any moment. Appreciating them while they're there is important. That's why I never, ever leave the house without telling everyone in my family that I love them. And I try to breathe in all the moments of joy we have along the way, no matter how small they might be. These moments put in perspective not only how important it is to take time with family and friends and to have gratitude for the good things in our lives but also how important it is to live a life that matters and to do work that has meaning.

As a leader, compassion is one of the most valuable skills we can have. Being able to put ourselves in someone else's shoes, to try to understand the world from that person's perspective, or at a minimum, to listen and learn more about that perspective, is critical to gaining trust as a leader, no matter your cause.

ASSUME THE BEST

It's easy to say that compassion is a critical leadership skill, and harder to be consistently compassionate in practice. I'm better at being compassionate at work, but it doesn't always come easily to me in all aspects of life—especially driving. I'm ashamed to admit it, but I'm one of those people who will mutter to myself angrily if someone turns without a signal, or waits too long to go after the light turns green. I can be heard saying embarrassing things like, "That person has no clue how to drive!" When Ben Rattray, the founder and CEO of Change.org, is in the car with me, he reminds me to have compassion even when I'm frustrated. "What if that person just came from the hospital and learned a loved one was dying?" or "What if they just found out they lost their job?" I know he is exaggerating to make a point, but actually, *he has a point*. It's a good reminder that you just never know the circumstances that someone else is living in.

Change.org has a Golden Rule equivalent: "Assume the best." It's a reminder that we can't fully understand others' intentions. There is a lot of research describing what social psychologists call the "Fundamental Attribution Error"—that people often ascribe the negative actions of others to innate characteristics, i.e., "who they are" rather than considering situational variables. And not surprisingly, we tend to do the exact opposite when interpreting our own behavior. While we should certainly be clear about how someone's actions affected us, it is also helpful to start from a place of compassion and not make assumptions about someone's intent without asking about it first.

If, instead, we had compassion for the people around us, assuming the best of their intentions, we could develop stronger long-term relationships with less conflict and reach better outcomes at the same time. I've also heard this concept referred to as "Most Respectful Interpretation" (MRI), and Brené Brown refers to it as the "hypothesis of generosity," the most generous interpretation you can make about someone's intentions, words, or actions.

Assuming the best, or using the hypothesis of generosity, also allows us to be a bit easier on ourselves, too. My friend Kate Gamble Dickman wrote one of the most beautiful posts I've ever read after the death of her younger brother Scott in early 2017. It was such a touching and emotional piece about grief, her brother, and the support of family and friends. In my favorite part, she told this story about getting back to the hotel after the service to celebrate Scott's life and realizing that every time she had hugged someone, her Spanx were showing. As she wrote, "After the celebration, I came back to our hotel room, spent. I realized that each time I raised my arms up to hug someone, my dress would ride up and you could see my Spanx. This made me laugh. I was hugging people all night. I'd hug two people at once. And my sweet little vulnerable, elastic, proverbial underbelly was exposed to all those folks. I'm so glad it was. My eyes were glossy and wet, and my Spanx were out there. There was no filtering, no protecting myself or others, no posturing. My Spanx were showing from feeling safe, from all that love, from holding onto the moment. From celebrating forty years of Scott."

We're all wearing Spanx—literally or figuratively, the coverings that hide our fears and insecurities—and the world would be a much better place if we could love and assume the best of each other and ourselves, even with our Spanx showing.

BRING LIFE INTO YOUR WORK

If you start with the premise that we'll build stronger teams when we first build stronger relationships with the people on them, you can apply several techniques I learned from the social organizers at Change.org to build stronger connections between people in more traditional work environments. It is common in social organizing for people to start by learning about each other and building deep and authentic relationships that help the group navigate challenges together. This is starting to happen in more and more organizations, from schools to companies. Sometimes this is done in ways that may seem "touchy-feely" or over the top to people who are part of more traditional organizations, but after integrating many of them at Change.org, I can say that we won over even the most skeptical of engineers and businesspeople. Here are a few examples of the types of exercises I've found effective:

- **Lifelines:** Break people into small groups, and ask everyone to describe three to five key moments or events in their lives that have influenced who they are today. It's an amazing way to break down the barriers between people and gain a deeper understanding of one another. These conversations are kept strictly confidential between the group members and, as a result, build enormous trust. I've heard stories about dealing with racism and the deaths of loved ones, recollections about inspiring mentors, unusual job opportunities, and more. It's a great way to deepen the relationships among your team.

- **Storytelling:** Building upon the lifeline exercise, encourage people to tell a meaningful story about their life in front of a larger group. One of the most memorable sessions we ever had at a company retreat was to hold a storytelling night in front of a campfire. Ten people from the company had volunteered to tell a powerful story from their lives in front of the whole company, which they had rehearsed beforehand. The stories we heard that night had us laughing and sobbing and appreciating the courage of the people who were willing to share so much of themselves. And their willingness to be exposed made everyone more willing to be open with each other.

- **Appreciations:** One of the most effective techniques I have seen to build trust within a group is appreciations. At the end of a project or an off-site meeting, we ask the group to share things they appreciate about each other. We go around the circle, giving each person a few minutes to be appreciated. The rest of the group can chime in with reasons why they appreciate that person, ideally using specific examples. The whole group isn't required to speak, but I've found there are usually more people who want to talk than time available. Don't get me wrong: it's awkward to be publicly appreciated by people. It's not something that most of us have experienced or are comfortable with. But it is also extremely moving. We so rarely take the time to tell others in our lives why we appreciate and admire them that when we do, it's unexpectedly powerful.

These types of activities build deeper and more meaningful relationships among coworkers, which then helps you work more effectively together. I've noticed that it helps with conflict resolution in particular; the stronger the foundational relationship between two people, the more easily these conflicts are resolved or avoided altogether. And knowing more about their colleagues helps people assume the best, as we discussed earlier. In fact, lots of people on my teams will tell you that when they come to me with an issue they are having with a colleague, my advice is "first, go have a beer" (or a cup of tea, you get the idea). If you can get to know someone first, then everything after that just comes more easily.

I've met some people who are skeptical that these techniques could work in their organization. Often, they tell me that they think these are great ideas and that they see how they could work inside a social change company, but that they couldn't work elsewhere. I strongly disagree. If we could get engineers and accountants to appreciate these activities, they can work anywhere. Tools that build deeper understanding between people add value to teams of any kind, from universities to traditional businesses to sports teams. After all, underneath our protective Spanx, we are all just human.

TAKE ONE FOR THE TEAM

ONE FINAL WAY to build trust has stayed with me since my rowing days. (Yes, I promise this is the last time I'll bring up rowing.) If you read the *Urban Dictionary* entry for *coxswain*, you'll learn that "upon winning a race, the coxswain is thrown into the (often very dirty) water." Literally, it says that—"the (often very dirty) water."

This is, unfortunately, true.

In the same way American football players throw Gatorade on their coach after the Super Bowl, rowers throw their coxswains in the water after a win. I am proud to say I have been thrown into many of the dirtiest lakes and rivers on the east and west coasts of the United States.

In the ultimate act of trust, rowers do not see where they are going—they trust their coxswain to steer them, encourage them, and push them to be better as individuals and as a team. And in return for this trust, and their extremely hard work, they ask the coxswain to "take one for the team." Throwing the coxswain in the water provides an outlet for celebration and release.

It's the same for all leaders. Sometimes the best way to build trust and loyalty is to let yourself be the butt of a joke or embarrass yourself for the good of the team. There are many times I have agreed to things that allow my team to celebrate and have fun at my expense. I have done everything from playing the cackling wicked witch in a company musical (yes, a company musical) to letting the team vote on which Halloween costume I would wear (one year a purple unicorn onesie and an-

other year a giant hamburger). Haven't we all been inspired by leaders who've done these things? I've seen great leaders dress up and perform as Justin Timberlake or get tattoos of their company logos. And an increasing amount of research shows that humor is an effective tool to increase trust and build bonds at work because it sparks a release of oxytocin, a hormone that is associated with social bonding. In fact, some business schools are offering classes in humor, such as Humor: Serious Business, by Stanford professors Jennifer Aaker and Naomi Bagdonas.

So as you think about how to build trust and support from those who join your team, let them throw you in the metaphorical lake once in a while.

Getting your team working effectively together is a key step in driving your movement forward. And as your movement continues to grow, you'll likely face one of the toughest challenges any successful movement eventually encounters: criticism. Knowing how to deal with inevitable opposition and even use it to your advantage can make all the difference in keeping your movement alive and thriving.

6

DON'T DRINK THE HATERADE

Using criticism as an advantage

Don't feed the trolls; you are not a jackass whisperer.

—Scott Stratten

PART OF THE PACKAGE

WHETHER YOU'RE TRYING to build a thriving company, write a new law, or launch a new program in your organization or community, you are going to face criticism, especially if you're successful. If you're trying to change something, it's just part of the package. It may be from people who don't agree with what you're trying to accomplish, or those who may agree with *what* you're trying to do but not *how* you're doing it. Sometimes, people may just want to take you down a notch. Criticism may also contain valid suggestions from people who want to help you improve. And feedback from others may indeed be a gift, even if it feels uncomfortable, which we'll talk more about in this chapter. Nevertheless, if you want to start a movement, you need to be prepared to face criticism, both the helpful kind and the less than helpful kind. In the words of Amazon founder and CEO Jeff Bezos, "If you absolutely can't tolerate critics, then don't do anything new or interesting."

There are two distinct types of criticism you may face on your journey to leading change: genuine and constructive feedback that has the potential to help you improve, and commentary from "haters" that is just meant to drag you down, often referred to as "trolling." We'll tackle them both. Note that sometimes even feedback that comes in the first category of "helpful" may not always be presented in the kindest way. As an example, some people I have talked to who are regularly in the public eye through their roles in the media try to separate the feedback about the "what they are doing" from the feedback on "who they are." They will listen to feedback about what they are doing or saying even when presented through trolling because it might represent a valid alternate opinion, whereas they will ignore feedback about their appearance, their background, and anything else irrelevant to their message.

Before we talk more about the different strategies for managing haters versus genuine constructive feedback, remember that you're in control of your reaction to criticism. Research shows that the amygdala triggers a fight-or-flight response when we receive negative feedback, making us feel threatened. And in fact, small amounts of negative information can cause us to react even more strongly than we do to larger amounts of positive information, a phenomenon known as "negativity bias." Even though our brains tend to have this same threatened reaction to criticism, we don't have to just sit back and be a slave to our amygdalas. Research has shown that by thinking positively, we can actively shift the ratio of positive to negative information in our brains and reduce the fight-or-flight reaction we have to criticism. One of the mechanisms that helps with this is to remind ourselves what we have to be grateful for. When *New York Times* writer Tony Schwartz did this, he found it worked surprisingly well: "[A]fter just a couple of minutes, I was not only feeling remarkably better, but also far more able to concentrate on the task at hand. It's a simple concept: we construct our internal reality—our experience of the world—in large part by where we put our attention. More often than we recognize, we can make that choice consciously and intentionally. Doing so influences not just how we feel, but also how we perform, individually and collaboratively. It turns out that cultivating positive emotions such as joy, contentment, interest, pride and love pays huge dividends."

REMEMBER THE ARMY BEHIND YOU

ONE WAY TO overcome the cruelty of haters is to build enough positivity around us to dwarf the negative reactions we do receive—to overcome our own negativity bias. Nearly every petition starter I spoke to told me that when their energy lagged or they felt overwhelmed by negative comments on social media, reading the supportive comments people had written as their reasons for signing the petition gave them inspiration to keep fighting their fight. On tough days, remembering that there was an army behind them, or around them, right there on their petition—good people who had added their signatures and even shared their own stories about why they'd signed—was what made all the difference. The positive energy of these comments outweighed the negative energy of any hatred they were receiving. It's a perfect example of how small actions really do matter.

Merna Forster, from Ottawa, Canada, is a writer and historian who led a successful national campaign calling for a woman to be put on the Canadian currency. For her, the campaign was not simply about women on banknotes. Rather, it was about the symbolism of making sure that women are recognized for their contributions to society, in part by ensuring that images of women appear alongside images of men. Merna's was a long campaign, lasting from 2013 to 2016, and it garnered some harsh criticism. "I was surprised, actually, that people would write nasty posts," Merna told me, explaining that people would criticize her on social media, and directly via the contact e-mail on her website. "I don't really have a very tough skin, so I found that very hard to take. It was like they were personally attacking me. They also personally attacked me on radio phone-in shows. That was what I disliked the most. Generally men would say some really nasty things, like, 'The only women who belong on banknotes are topless ones.' Or they would post nasty pictures of body parts. Eventually I did not read the comments on the articles anymore because it was just too disheartening. What I would do instead is go back to the comments on the Change.org website and read the messages of support."

During the many ups and downs of her campaign, Merna found true inspiration reading the comments left by those who had signed her petition. In fact, those "voices" acted like a virtual support group when she needed one most. She even printed them out and carried them around with her. "The fact that people can post their reasons for signing was one of the best things about the whole process," she told me. "All of a sudden, you're not alone anymore. They would say things like, 'We need these role models' and 'My little girl needs to see women on banknotes and so does my son, actually.' Now I had this support group and all these thousands of people are signing, sending words of encouragement. Later on, when I got discouraged, it was reading these reasons for signing that kept me going."

And it was good that Merna kept up her fight, even when it got tough and she faced hard and personally hateful criticism. In 2016, Bill Morneau, the Canadian minister of finance, announced that in 2018, Viola Desmond would be the first woman on a Canadian banknote other than the queen of England. Viola Desmond was a black businesswoman from Nova Scotia, known for sparking the civil rights movement in Canada when she was convicted, jailed, and fined for refusing to leave the whites-only section of a movie theater in 1946. As Morneau said in his decision-maker response on Change.org, "As she takes her place on our $10 bill, Viola will remind all of us, and future generations, that big change can start with small moments of dignity and bravery." Amen.

It was one of my most surprising takeaways from writing this book—each individual comment of support on these petitions meant so much to the people that started them. If we each knew how much our words could matter, wouldn't we make the extra effort to write or say a few kind words more often?

So build an army. Even if you don't have a petition where your army can sign on, find those people that are behind you and give them a way to join you. You can use other types of technology, like group chats or online groups, or create a team that gets together in person if your issue is local. Your army doesn't have to agree with every move you make, and some of your supporters may also have suggestions and feedback for you that will make you better, but find people who *believe* in you and in your cause. Put more positive around you than negative, and it can boost you up, even amid the cruelest of trolls.

HATERS GONNA HATE

WHILE MOST PEOPLE who try to change things anticipate some criticism and negative feedback, not everyone expects the tsunami of "haterade" that may be headed their way. However, in today's world, where information rapidly spreads through the Internet and social media, anyone who puts themselves in the public eye should be prepared for the fact that both genuine feedback and trolling will be part of the process.

McKenna Pope of Garfield, New Jersey, was just thirteen when she petitioned Hasbro, one of the largest toy companies in the world, to market its Easy-Bake Oven to boys as well as girls by producing it in gender-neutral colors. Inspired by her younger brother Gavin, who loved to cook but was too embarrassed to use the toy oven he'd gotten for Christmas because it seemed like it was just for girls, McKenna posted a video and started a petition to persuade the company to stop marketing solely to girls in their television ads and through their stereotypical product colors. As she explained in her TED talk, "Hasbro marketed them specifically to girls. . . . They would only feature girls on the boxes or in the commercials, and there would be flowery prints all over the ovens and it would be in bright pink and purple, very gender-specific colors to females, right? So it kind of was sending a message that only girls are supposed to cook; boys aren't. And this discouraged my brother a lot. He thought that he wasn't supposed to want to be a chef, because that was something that girls did. Girls cooked; boys didn't, or so was the message that Hasbro was sending."

McKenna's actions worked. After getting over 45,000 signatures on her petition, Hasbro invited her to come to its corporate headquarters in Pawtucket, Rhode Island, so she could see its new product line of unisex designs and new colors: black, silver, and blue. The visit, she said, "was literally one of the best moments of my life. It was like *Willy Wonka and the Chocolate Factory*. That thing was amazing." But just as she was basking in her unlikely success, something quite unexpected happened. She started to receive a lot of hateful comments, too. McKenna says, "People online, and sometimes even in real life, were disrespectful to me and my family and talked about how the whole thing was a waste of time, and it really discouraged me."

To deal with the online negativity, McKenna did two things—first, she took control by exposing her haters in her TED talk—reading out mean tweets she'd received to prove that she had the power in this relationship: "from @Liquidsore29: *Disgusting liberal moms making their sons gay*; from @Whiteboy77AGS: *People always need something to bitch about*; and from Jeffrey Gutierrez: *OMG, shut up. You just want money and attention.*"

And then she learned to let it go. It didn't take long for McKenna to realize that criticism was just part of making change and that it didn't have to stop her from continuing to fight for what she believed in. She repeated the mantra "Haters gonna hate" to herself as a way to help keep going. She made her TED audience even say it with her. As she told them, "Let your haters hate, and make your change, because I know you can. You can take what you believe in and turn it into a cause and change it. And . . . you can use that spark that you have within you and turn it into a fire."

As McKenna found, you can choose to control your attitude toward haters and not give them power over you. As the famous quote widely attributed to Eleanor Roosevelt says, "No one can make you feel inferior without your consent."

However, if trolling becomes repeated harassment or includes threats of physical violence, you should report those people to ensure that you are not in any physical danger. Remember that there are tools in nearly all technology platforms to let you mute, block, and report people, and you should use them as you see fit.

PROVE YOUR CRITICS WRONG

AS A LONG-TIME tech executive, Kara Goldin knew when she left AOL that she wanted to find work that would make a difference. "I felt like I needed to do something that had some sort of purpose," she told me, assuming she would land in the nonprofit space. But what happened next—starting Hint Water, a beverage company and a whole new category in the beverage industry (flavored water)— surprised even her. "In a million years I would have never thought that was what I was going to do next."

Like many entrepreneurs, Kara's business idea emerged while trying to solve a problem of her own. In her case, it was that no matter how much she exercised and how healthfully she was eating, she couldn't seem to lose the weight she'd gained after the birth of her third child. While searching for her next role, Kara was also examining everything she was eating and drinking. Unsure of whether she had a hormone imbalance or was showing signs of being prediabetic, Kara decided to further moderate her diet before turning to medication. That's when she noticed something she hadn't been aware of before: she'd been drinking a lot of Diet Coke and had never fully understood the ingredients and the effects that artificial sweeteners have on the body. Once she took a closer look, she decided to completely stop drinking diet soda and started drinking plain water instead. "It's really as simple as that." The result of that single but important switch was huge. Over the course of the next two weeks, she lost over twenty pounds; in six months almost fifty pounds had melted away.

But after a year of drinking plain water, Kara craved a more interesting beverage—something like what she was making for herself at home—water with sliced fruit in it. "The key thing for me was figuring out how to drink more water, and I realized that drinking water for me, and for many people I talked to along the way, was really hard because it was so boring. So one day I went to Whole Foods and I said to the person that worked there, 'I'd really like to find this product, which is water with just a little bit of fruit to give it some flavor. Can you help find it on the shelf?' He told me about this 'great product' called Vitamin Water, which at that time probably had more sugar in it than a can of Coke. A few more conversations with him led me to the growing sense that most people weren't aware of how much sugar and artificial sweeteners were in the beverages they were drinking and how much those ingredients were adversely affecting their health. Finally I said to the Whole Foods guy, 'I should just go develop this product myself.' And he kind of laughed at me and said, 'Okay, lady, great. I'm sure you're gonna go develop the product.' So I said to him, 'What do you need from me to actually develop the product?' And he said, 'Well, you know, you need a shelf life, you need a name of the product. And let me know when you develop that.'"

He laughed her off. He thought it was funny and assumed it was unlikely, if not impossible.

Boy did she prove him wrong.

Even though the timing wasn't ideal—she was still interviewing for tech jobs and had just found out she was pregnant with her fourth child—she told her husband what she wanted to do. Despite some initial doubts about entering a new category they knew nothing about, her husband helped her with getting the product ready to launch. "It was a crazy timeline of around six months to actually produce a product front to back," she said, "and I was running a couple weeks behind and then finally got my product the day before I was having a planned C-section." Kara and her husband delivered the first ten cases themselves to the Whole Foods close to where they lived on the morning of the *day* her C-section was scheduled to happen.

Though she wasn't sure that Whole Foods had actually put the product on the shelves, the next morning she got a call in the hospital room: the first batch had completely sold out. "He said we had to get over there ASAP because we wouldn't have space on the shelf anymore unless we got more product in to fill it." Kara had indeed successfully made a product she could sell at Whole Foods, despite their skepticism.

Kara faced many more obstacles, from needing to find a way to make Hint Water shelf stable with no preservatives, to persuading grocery stores to create space for a product that didn't fit into an existing category. She also faced more critics. At one low point, she considered selling her company to one of the large beverage companies, who she thought could take the company further than she could, given all their expertise. On a phone call with a senior executive at that company, she broached the idea to him, and he said, "Sweetie, I don't want your company because Americans love sweet. And this will never be a large company."

Once she got past the fact that he had called her "sweetie," she saw that his skepticism left open a huge opportunity for her and for Hint Water. Kara realized then that the two companies would be so different and that she needed to stay the course, because if she didn't, then a product like Hint would not exist. When people were telling her she was wrong, she actually viewed that as an opportunity. As she told me, "I kept challenging the theory—primarily because people couldn't actually answer my questions." Kara found that it's common to listen to others who have experience and assume they must be right because they've been at a big, "awesome" company or have years of experience, but that often those people can't think as creatively as an outsider about what is possible.

So Kara proved another skeptic wrong. Twelve years later, Hint Water has grown to become a $100 million company, and it's still growing, expanding beyond beverages into new categories, having become a movement about wellness. When Kara faced some precancerous skin issues, she realized that oxybenzone and parabens in her sunscreen were exacerbating them. So she decided to launch a paraben-free sunscreen, using the essences from the fruit that they use for Hint water to scent the sunscreens. While many in the beverage industry thought that it was crazy for Hint to launch a sunscreen, Kara believed that Hint customers were so passionate about the brand and the movement it had created that they would buy products beyond beverages. And they did. When Hint initially launched the sunscreen, 60 percent of all consumers who had purchased Hint Water online in the past twelve months also bought the sunscreen. Yet again, Kara is proving her critics wrong.

LEVERAGE THE NAYSAYERS

ANOTHER WAY TO approach your critics is to see if you can actually use their expertise for advice. Mary Lou Jepsen is one of the brightest technical minds of our time, with a career including roles as a professor at MIT Media Lab and leading teams at both Google X and Facebook's Oculus team. She is known for being able to create things that seem impossible, such as the one-hundred-dollar solar-powered laptop she and her team built at One Laptop per Child. Which is why it's so ironic that when she was a child, her parents didn't allow her the same intellectual curiosity and freedom that her brothers had. "My brothers got to do things I didn't get to do. And even when I got to their same age, I still didn't get to do them. And I hated that. They got to stay out later, they got to go on trips, and they got electronics kits. I'm now one of the top electronic engineers in the world but I wasn't even allowed to touch those kits," she told me. "I thought it was utterly unfair. But I ended up majoring in electrical engineering and then I got the World Technology Hardware Award a couple of years ago. It's sort of funny that I wasn't allowed to touch the electronics kit growing up, but I wasn't." Sometimes people who say "you can't" end up fueling your deepest ambitions. Mary Lou may not have been allowed to touch her brothers' electronics kit, but those early limitations obviously didn't stop her—among her many honors she's been named one of *Time* magazine's "Time 100" (one of the 100 most influential people in the world) and a CNN top 10 thinker.

As Mary Lou progressed in her life and career, she learned that one way to get the most out of those who don't believe in you is to actively solicit critical feedback from those most likely to find fault in your ideas. When she founded One Laptop per Child (OLPC), she told me that even though there was high demand for the product (an inexpensive, low-power, sunlight-readable laptop) from heads of state around the world who wanted it for students in their countries, there were still many people who never believed it would be possible to build the product. "I met with the heads of the large Asian tech companies because I wanted their help," she told me. "And I remember my first meeting with the chairman of a very large company in Asia. I went into the big boardroom and it was just me from OLPC and ten people on the other side of the table: the chairman in the center was flanked by the EVPs on each side. And they just started laughing at me. Think of the dynamic: I'm a white woman with all these Asian men and they just started laughing at me and telling me, 'Hahaha, it'll never work.'"

But instead of giving in to their condescension, Mary Lou did something remarkable: she managed to figure out a way, right there on the spot, to leverage the negativity of her naysayers and turn it to her advantage. "I found myself pulling out a notebook and saying, 'Okay, tell me why it won't work?' And they just started spouting off things and over the course of an hour and a half they came up with twenty-three different reasons it wouldn't work. I was just dutifully taking notes, very much in the gender dynamic of note-taking. At the end, they were very pleased, and I said, 'Okay, we've got twenty-three things here. I have seventeen of these already solved. These new six things are really good. You guys know a lot about this. You're one of the largest manufacturers of consumer electronics in the world. This is amazing. Thank you. So here's an idea: Can I take these back to the team to work on and then I'll come back to you in a few months as we have answers and see if you can find any other problems with our plan?'"

And that's exactly what Mary Lou did. The tech companies continued to take meetings with her, and each time they did, she gained helpful ideas from their top talent in laptop design, consumer electronics, and software design. "They could debug the problems in their head before we spent the money and the time building the prototype," she told me. In the end, the people who told her she wouldn't be able to achieve her goal were the ones who actually helped her get there. By listening to what they were saying and availing herself of the group's expert opinions, she was able to anticipate problems and find solutions to them much more quickly than she would have had she not sought out their help.

TRY THE BEAR HUG

NOLAND CHAMBLISS ON the communications team at Change .org coined the term "Bear Hug" as an approach to conflict resolution. Even when you are being attacked, if you approach your attacker with an oversize amount of love and understanding, you may be able to resolve your issue more effectively than if you get defensive.

There is a classic example of the Bear Hug in a wonderful Story-Corps piece that originally aired on NPR's *Latino USA* from 2008. A young man, Julio Diaz, tells the story of how he is mugged at knife-point on his way home by a teenager. In addition to giving the teen his wallet, as demanded, Julio also offered him something he hadn't asked for. "Hey, wait a minute," he told the teen before he ran off. "You forgot something. If you're going to be robbing people for the rest of the night, you might as well take my coat to keep you warm." Ultimately, the two ended up in conversation over dinner at Julio's favorite diner, where—seeing the kindness Julio showed everyone from the manager to the dishwashers to the waiters when they all stopped by their table to say hello—the teen realized he could approach life differently. He gave Julio back his wallet and also surrendered his knife in return for dinner, a small amount of money, and for the unexpected show of kindness, which was so rare in this young man's life.

• • •

A FEW YEARS ago, shortly after I started working at Change.org, the site was attacked by a computer scientist from Spain who was using a particular technique to add fake signatures to a Change.org petition and take screenshots of them. Then he'd post them on Twitter more quickly than we could remove them. Although we had tools that would catch and remove any fraudulent signatures, some would take minutes to be removed and others could take up to twenty-four hours. (Change.org has also improved these tools significantly since that incident.) It was a crisis for us at the time, especially in Spain, where the local press was following the story closely.

We debated various approaches we could take at the time, including getting a large portion of our tech team involved to go "head to head" with the attacker to try to stop him with a technical approach. Instead, Benjamin Joffe-Walt (BJW), then the VP of communications, suggested we try the Bear Hug. In this case, offering love and understanding to our attacker meant getting BJW on the first flight to Spain to meet the spammer in person. It was counterintuitive to many of us, and I remember thinking at the time that it was a really unusual approach that would be unlikely to happen at other tech companies. But it seemed worth a try.

The spammer lived on a small island in Spain, and BJW went there in person to hear what he had to say and to listen directly to his concerns. It turned out that he was upset because he thought it was easy for people to add fake signatures to Change.org petitions and was concerned that a specific petition that was large in Spain at the time might have illegitimate signatures on it. He had tried to prove that was possible, which was what started this incident. When we went there and explained our system to him (at a high level, since it's not good practice to give spammers the technical details of your fraud prevention), he then understood that while individual fake signatures could take up to twenty-four hours to remove, that any fake signatures that come in bulk are caught almost immediately. More important, though, he felt listened to and respected by our effort to talk to him, and especially to meet him in person. The next thing we knew, we were getting photos of BJW and our spammer drinking beers together, arms around each other in a Spanish bar, and the spam attack had stopped. Bear Hug: 1, spam: 0.

• • •

TRYING TO UNDERSTAND those who are attacking you isn't easy, but it's often the best way to make your cause stronger. Hearing your critics out allows you to find ways to welcome even those who are most dismissive or have perspectives most different from yours. It requires you to step outside the pain that their actions cause and try to imagine what's behind them. Is it possible that they're struggling with something, too? People do not come out of the womb as haters and trolls. There must be something in their life that has led to the anger, pain, or fear that causes them to be so hateful to others. And if we can work to understand what's behind the hate, then maybe it's possible to eliminate it. As Nelson Mandela said, "No one is born hating another person because of the color of his skin, or his background, or his religion. People must learn to hate, and if they can learn to hate, they can be taught to love, for love comes more naturally to the human heart than its opposite." *Are you able to love the haters*—to show love to people who are showing you the exact opposite?

One of the most astounding examples I've ever heard about on how to approach a hater with compassion and curiosity instead of anger and fear is also one of the most improbable. As Eli Saslow wrote in a piece for the *Washington Post*, the story begins when students at New College in Sarasota, Florida, discovered the true identity of twenty-one-year-old transfer student Derek Black. The "quirky" guy with long red hair and a cowboy hat wasn't just a fellow history student who watched movies with them in the dorm; he was an avowed white supremacist, the son of Don Black, whose website

Stormfront was the first white nationalist site on the Internet. Derek had started a version of Stormfront especially for young readers, and David Duke, former Imperial Wizard of the Ku Klux Klan, was his godfather.

When word of Derek's political beliefs spread on campus via an online forum, the message thread grew to over a thousand comments, including this one: "Derek Black: white supremacist, radio host . . . New College student???" the post read. "How do we as a community respond?" While many responses were understandably harsh—"He chooses to be a racist public figure. We choose to call him a racist in public"—a feeling that censure and exposure weren't enough in this case seemed to be growing: "Maybe he's trying to get away from a life he didn't choose." Something else seemed to be at play: a sense that a deeper understanding would be necessary. "Ostracizing Derek won't accomplish anything," one student wrote, while another commented, "We have a chance to be real activists and actually affect one of the leaders of white supremacy in America. This is not an exaggeration. It would be a victory for civil rights."

That's when Matthew Stevenson, the only Orthodox Jewish student at New College, did something extraordinary: he invited Derek Black to Shabbat dinner at his apartment, a weekly Friday night tradition he had started and that involved friends who were almost all non-Jews. According to the *Washington Post:*

> Matthew decided his best chance to affect Derek's thinking was not to ignore him or confront him, but simply to include him. "Maybe he'd never spent time with a Jewish person before," Mat-

thew remembered thinking. It was the only social invitation Derek had received since returning to campus, so he agreed to go. The Shabbat meals had sometimes included eight or 10 students, but this time only a few showed up. "Let's try to treat him like anyone else," Matthew remembered instructing them. Derek arrived with a bottle of wine. Nobody mentioned white nationalism or the forum, out of respect for Matthew. Derek was quiet and polite, and he came back the next week and then the next, until after a few months, nobody felt all that threatened, and the Shabbat group grew back to its original size.

Derek explained to me in a recent interview that the Shabbat dinner remained a safe space, one where white nationalism was never discussed and where Derek could build trusting relationships with people who had different backgrounds and views. Eventually, in other settings, those new trusted friends were able to question Derek about his beliefs, which led to Derek drafting a response on the student forum in which many of his previously held views appeared to have softened. As the *Washington Post* reported, Derek said, "It's been brought to my attention that people might be scared or intimidated or even feel unsafe here because of things said about me," he began. "I wanted to try to address these concerns publicly, as they absolutely should not exist. I do not support oppression of anyone because of his or her race, creed, religion, gender, socioeconomic status or anything similar." The post was leaked to the Southern Poverty Law Center (SPLC), one of the focuses of his father's hatred, and so began one of the most incredible public reversals of racist ideology. As Derek continued to explain his changing views on the student forum, it was clear that he was undergoing a change of heart.

And indeed, by the fall of 2016, as Donald Trump won the electoral college and became president-elect of the United States, Derek's remarkable ideological transformation was complete, evidenced by his extraordinary op-ed for the *New York Times*, titled "Why I Left White Nationalism." In it he wrote:

Several years ago, I began attending a liberal college where my presence prompted huge controversy. Through many talks with devoted and diverse people there—people who chose to invite me into their dorms and conversations rather than ostracize me—I began to realize the damage I had done. Ever since, I have been trying to make up for it. . . .

For me, the conversations that led me to change my views started because I couldn't understand why anyone would fear me. I thought I was only doing what was right and defending those I loved. . . .

If I had not changed, I would have been jubilant after this election and more certain than ever that anxiety from a shrinking white majority would result in the election of more people who tap into this simple narrative. Now I'm convinced this doesn't have to be our destiny.

By showing love to one of the most extreme haters in the nation, Matthew Stevenson and his friends were able to truly transform Derek's views and perhaps change the course of history. Changing the mind of someone so influential will have ripple effects far beyond shifting the opinions of one individual. We are at a more divided crossroads in history than we've seen in many, many years, and we do have the power to have an impact on where we go from here. Derek told me that there were two critical elements that led to him changing his mind about white nationalism. The first was hearing people express their own values strongly and condemn his hateful behavior, specifically by explaining how it had personally caused them pain. The second was having people who were willing to talk, listen, and build trust with him rather than immediately expressing anger—reacting with outrage to the behavior but not to him as a person. If, as Derek says, we can focus on "honest listening on both sides," we each have the ability to make a real difference.

EVEN THE BEST ATHLETES HAVE COACHES

WHILE THERE ARE haters and trolls out there, if we are open to it, we will see that much of the feedback we receive may actually take the form of suggestions for how we can improve our ideas and be more successful in our efforts to pursue the causes that matter to us. People who push us often do make us better. We may not always agree with the feedback, and it may not always be presented in an ideal way, but if we stay in the right mind-set, we can see this feedback as the gift that it is.

I had the chance to meet Ken Blanchard, bestselling author and leadership expert, while I was in business school at Cornell. Among many of his lessons that stayed with me is this one: "Even the best athletes in the world have coaches." It's an apt way to think about how to receive constructive feedback. Now, whenever someone gives me a critique or makes a suggestion about a different approach I could take, rather than get upset, I try to embrace my inner Steve Young or Joe Montana. (I grew up in San Francisco, and instead of teen pop stars, I had posters of 49ers quarterbacks on my walls.) If we want to be really good at something, and especially if we want to be one of the best at something, we have to acknowledge that other people may have ideas that can help us improve. And coaches don't have to be "better" than you, they just have to have a different perspective and set of experiences that make *you* better. Michael Jordan's coach wasn't better than him at shooting three pointers, and Serena Williams's coach doesn't have a better serve. But they offer feedback that has value.

Even my teen idol, Steve Young, had people who suggested plays to him, gave him advice on his form, and generally made him a better player. And it would be horribly arrogant of me to assume that I could not improve by listening to the ideas of others. If we take constructive feedback as negative criticism and refuse to listen to it, then we deny ourselves the opportunity to grow.

That's not to say that accepting constructive feedback is always easy, especially when it comes in large amounts or at moments of particular uncertainty. In 2016 Change.org went through a challenging time as we worked to find a revenue model that would help us get to sustainability faster, lowering the need for continued outside investment while preserving our ability to continue our rapid audience growth and increasing global impact. As part of the process around the business model shift and the drive toward sustainability, we had to make the difficult decision to let go of some of our respected team members. As the president of the company at that time, I felt responsible for decisions that had led us to the place where we had to make these difficult choices. I felt a lot of guilt over having to let go of people who were clearly talented, many of whom I had personally recruited, knowing the challenges this would cause for them. Though I knew it was necessary to take these actions to preserve the company's ability to achieve its mission and to continue to serve the hundreds of millions of people who use the Change.org platform, it was really tough to do.

Amid what was already a lot of self-criticism, I had to think about how I would show up as a leader in that moment. I knew my first step was to take responsibility and acknowledge the role I had played in what was a difficult time for many on the team. There were many different reactions from people about how we should process the situation. Some just wanted to move on and get back to business, to continue working hard on getting us where we needed to be. Many people who had worked in other tech companies or startups were familiar with this process, as it is somewhat core to the Silicon Valley mind-set—you make big bets in an effort to scale—sometimes they work well and lead to step-function changes in your business, and other times they just don't work. In those cases you "fail fast" and you move on. Other people in our organization, and especially those who came from social-organizing backgrounds, felt that it was important to unearth the reasons why we had gotten to the point of having to lose valued members of our team in the first place. They wanted to examine and reevaluate the ways that we worked, the ways that we shared information, and the ways that we made decisions in the company to see if there was something that we could do differently in the future to avoid getting into that situation again.

For me, that type of deep reflection, a kind of collective soul-searching, was a relatively new experience. We do have that concept in tech, often referred to as a postmortem, where when something breaks in a product, we go back and analyze why it happened and what we could do differently. But this was something deeper. People suggested having every single person in our organization contribute their feedback and ideas. That sounded pretty scary, especially when I knew this was a raw moment when people would likely be particularly critical. But perhaps this was when the feedback might also be most valuable. So IICDTICDA, I thought. Instead of caving in to my discomfort, I aimed to embrace my inner athlete and said, "Okay. Maybe there is something I can learn here." At a minimum I knew it would likely be good for people to be able to express frustration, disappointment, and other emotions they were feeling, and at its best, there would be meaningful ideas that came out of the process that could make me a better leader and make us a higher functioning organization.

Several people within the organization agreed to lead a process where they went about interviewing everyone throughout the company in small groups to find out what questions they had about what had happened and why, and their ideas about how they'd like us to work differently. They summarized what they had found and presented it to me and the rest of the company's leadership. Of course, in some ways it was hard to hear, but with the feedback came ideas for solutions. And the ideas were good. We were aligned on many, and there were also additional ideas they had that could make us better and that may not have occurred to me alone.

In the end, they had a great list of recommended solutions, almost every single one was feasible, and most of them were implemented. Many of the ideas also covered ways that people from across the company could contribute, making everyone feel like they were part of the solution. We were a much stronger company for having gone through that process, which was balanced and allowed everybody to be heard. In fact, though it seemed a bit scary up front, it far exceeded my expectations—yet another example of someone else's idea being better than my own—since I would not have recommended this process in the first place. Had I just been defensive about the feedback and shut down the discussion, I would never have been able to get around my blind spots, and our organization would have suffered for it.

And the world's best athletes take this approach, too. After winning a brutally hard Game 2 of the NBA Finals in June 2017, Stephen Curry, one of this generation's most talented basketball players, was asked how he felt about winning the game. Instead of celebrating being up 2–0 in the series or commending his teammates, his response was, "I can play better." And he probably can (though that may be debatable in his case). This is the response of a champion and of a great leader—someone who knows there is always room to be better. So whether your favorite athlete is Simone Biles, Muhammad Ali, or Joe Montana, embrace the pro athlete inside you and remember that we can always improve and that feedback from others can make us stronger than we can be on our own.

7

MOUNTAIN CLIMBING

Overcoming obstacles and failing well

*This thing that we call "failure" is not the falling down,
but the staying down.*

—MARY PICKFORD

PREPARE FOR THE WEATHER

WE START MOVEMENTS because we want to see big change, and that most likely involves overcoming big obstacles. One way to help get past obstacles is to remember that they are coming. There's a slide I use in a lot of presentations and talks that I give. On one side of the slide there's a picture of a grassy mountain on a sunny day, and I show a line pointing near the top, to the word "me." On the other side there's a photo of a steep, dangerous mountain on a dark and stormy day, and I show a line pointing to the very bottom, where it also reads "me."

This is how I describe to people what it feels like to be an entrepreneur. It's also how it feels to be a leader of any team or any movement. Either you're near the top of the mountain and it's sunny and you've brought a picnic lunch, or you're down at the bottom, with a storm

CREDIT FOR SUNNY MOUNTAIN SIDE: GUILHELM VELLUT
CREDIT FOR STORMY MOUNTAIN SIDE: AU_EARS

brewing, carrying a heavy pack, and you're not sure you'll ever get to the top. These two metaphorical days rotate all the time. The highs and lows are in a constant state of flux. You don't suddenly and miraculously get past all the punishing challenges and reach eternal sunshine every day after that. Rather, it's a never-ending cycle of sunny to cloudy to sunny to cloudy, and hopefully back to sunny again.

The key to success is holding on to the belief that you'll have more sunny days than cloudy ones and to just keep climbing, every day, no matter what. Great leaders not only keep climbing on both types of days but also inspire their teams to climb with them. Because there will always be cloudy days, we should expect them, prepare for them, and surround ourselves with resources to get through them. Those cloudy days won't last forever, though; sunny days will come again and we should appreciate them when they do. It's important to keep climbing on the sunny days, too, and not to stop too long for the picnic lunch. Otherwise someone may come up behind you and pass you up.

When I led The Dealmap, there were many cloudy days. I often felt like the company was going to fail, especially in the first couple of years as a startup when we had to change the product and even the name of the company several times. And then more frequently, and especially after we finally hit on the right idea, we'd have days when it felt like the company was going to be awesome. Back and forth. Up and down. Highs and lows.

Ben Silbermann, the founder and CEO of Pinterest, has described this type of entrepreneurial leadership as the intersection between terror and joy, as he showed in the following slide from a keynote he gave in 2012 at the Alt Summit in Salt Lake City.

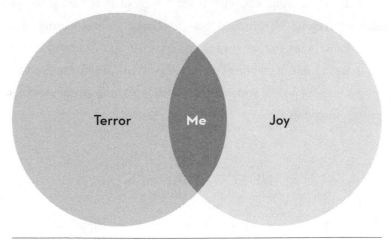

Ben Silbermann's Venn Diagram   ALT SUMMIT

I can relate. It's certainly not all rainbows and unicorns, and part of getting through the challenges is to be honest with each other that they exist so we don't feel so alone when we face them. If we can recognize that every other leader is facing the same fears and anxiety, then ours won't feel so bad. And as we'll see later in this chapter, often the challenges themselves have value—they make us stronger, and each one makes us more capable of handling the next. Plus, if you enjoy the process, you're inspired by the people you're working with, and you believe in what you're doing, then those sunny days of belief and persistence will help you get past the much bleaker ones.

David Dodson, a lecturer at the Stanford Graduate School of Business whom I am lucky to work with in teaching a case study about some of my experiences, makes another great point about "mountain climbing." He says, "The summit you will work so hard to reach only provides you with a better view of all the other mountains yet to climb." It is indeed true that the act of overcoming challenges both helps you see others you have yet to tackle *and* makes you more capable of tackling them. So keep climbing the mountain, bring a team of people you want to climb with, and remember that you are not alone.

THE *ROCKY* MOMENT

I'M A SUCKER for movies. And I mean really a sucker. I cry during nearly every movie I watch, including the animated ones, which is a running joke in my family. And I have a tendency to get so deeply pulled into the plot that my friends have seen me do ridiculous things like clap in the theater for a performance on film, or even wave good-bye to a character who is waving on-screen. I suppose it's because I truly believe in the power of art to tell stories and for those stories to teach lessons that are valuable in life.

So it's no surprise that I am especially inspired by those moments in movies and theater when someone is down and pulls themselves back up. I call it the *Rocky* Moment. You've lost one round, or two, or maybe every fight up until now, but you work harder, throw everything you have into it, get support and inspiration from others around you, and come back to win against the fiercest competitor. Or *The Martian* Moment, when you face a seemingly insurmountable challenge like bringing a stranded astronaut back from Mars before he dies, so you pull a talented team together, stumble through lots of failed ideas, and at the last possible minute, you come up with the one idea that just might work.

I believe these moments happen offscreen, too, in our daily lives. Some of them are just as dramatic as in the movies—from life-saving surgeries, to last-minute Hail Mary passes in professional sports, to feats of science that break new barriers, to campaigns that make massive global policy change. And some of these moments are smaller, like succeeding on a test we didn't think we'd pass or getting funding for a project we thought no one would support. Big or small, we all have those *Rocky* Moments when we work hard and achieve something no one thought was possible, sometimes not even ourselves.

It's not to say that there won't be failures along the way. In fact, the very *premise* of a *Rocky* Moment is that failures must come before success. If it isn't hard enough to warrant failures in the process of getting there, then it's likely not a big enough challenge. But as F. Scott Fitzgerald wrote, "You mustn't confuse a single failure with a final defeat." We can look at these smaller failures in our lives not as final defeat but rather as part of the path to ultimate success, and we can learn from those failures along the way to make us stronger and increase our chances of achieving our ultimate goal. To quote Rocky Balboa himself, "It ain't about how hard you hit. It's about how hard you can get hit and keep moving forward." If we see our lives as a series of *Rocky* Moments, we might just surprise ourselves with what we are able to accomplish. And the harder the fight, the sweeter the victory.

FESTIVAL OF FAILURE

ONCE WE ACKNOWLEDGE that there will be many failures on our path, the question is what we do with them. And though it might be cliché (and is likely cliché for a reason), what we should be doing, of course, is learning from our failures. But is it possible to really go big when we learn from failure? I mean really kick the shit out of learning from failure? I believe it is. And the way to do that is to not just casually think, "Boy, that didn't work," but rather to dig in, understand and document exactly *what* didn't work or *why* it didn't work. And if you really want to take it to the next level, then the best way to do that is to share it. I don't mean just mention it to someone else. I mean shout-it-from-the-rooftops share it, especially with people who are trying to solve the same problem as you. The more we know about each other's failures, the less likely we are to repeat them, and the faster we'll be able to move on toward finding solutions.

Thomas Edison is reported to have said, "I have not failed. I've just found 10,000 ways that won't work." And each of those 10,000 ways showed him something about what he might want to try or not try in the next experiment. He realized that he could get to solutions faster if he made mistakes faster and had more people working on the same problem. In fact, Edison's laboratory in West Orange, New Jersey, was the first full-fledged research and development lab ever created. The speed of getting through failures to ultimate success led Edison to create 1,093 new U.S. patents—one for every two weeks of his working career. Edison and the team at his lab were the ultimate expression of the "fail fast" mentality that is now so common in Silicon Valley and other innovation hubs around the world.

At Change.org we destigmatized failure by instituting something called the "Festival of Failure," a method to encourage people to share their failures in a way that others could learn from as well. It wasn't formalized in one single way across the company. Instead, each team adapted the idea to its own workflow. Some global or functional teams had a Festival of Failure section in each weekly team call in which people chimed in with recent failure examples. The engineering team, whose members do demos with each other every week to show what they've been working on, would periodically have their own "Festival of Failure" demos to show examples of mistakes they made or code they broke and what they learned. The festivals highlight failure as a learning opportunity without shaming people for mistakes. They help us recognize that we all have failures, especially when we are trying to do ambitious things. There is no shame in that. The only shame is in not sharing the failures we make so others can learn from and avoid them.

IT'S ONLY FAILURE IF YOU GO HOME

IN MY OWN experience as a startup founder, I learned in painful detail that failure is a necessary part of the process of building something. After nearly ten years moving up in the ranks at Yahoo!, I wanted to see if I could build a company from the ground up—a product that would solve an important user need, an outstanding team, and an inspiring company culture. I wanted to try my hand at being a CEO. While I was excited for the challenge, I had my fair share of apprehension. I knew that the possibility of failure with startups was extremely high. In fact, I remember reading a statistic in *The Book of Odds* that said I was more likely to report seeing a UFO (one out of 5.8 U.S. adults) than for my startup company to succeed (depending on what source you use, between one out of seven and one out of ten). Many of the people I knew told me how surprised they were that I was leaving an executive position at Yahoo! to lead this small company that didn't yet have a bulletproof product. I told myself rationally that even if I failed, I would be fine. I knew that with my previous experience I would be able to get another job afterward, so I wasn't putting myself financially at risk. I also knew I had family and friends who would support me no matter what; even if my business failed, they wouldn't see *me* as a failure. But while my rational mind said that all would be okay, there was still a nagging voice, deep inside, telling me I was afraid to fail. Nevertheless, my desire to build and create something new and to prove to myself I could at least give it a go won out.

So I jumped in. I joined a very small existing company rather than starting completely from scratch. I chose a company with people I thought I could learn from: incredible technical founder Chandu Thota, an engineer who had come from Microsoft, and experienced board chair Bill Harris, who had previously been the CEO of Intuit and PayPal. And I did learn so much from them and many others over the next several years. I also learned how hard it is to be an entrepreneur, and boy did I make a lot of mistakes, especially at the beginning.

When I first joined the company, a neighborhood social networking site called Fatdoor, I didn't like the name since it was hard to understand and I thought unappealing with the word "fat" in it. But my decision to rename it Center'd was arguably much worse. Leaving out the third *e* (because we couldn't afford to buy the domain with the proper spelling) and replacing it with an apostrophe was one of the worst ideas I've ever had. We couldn't even use the possessive form of our name in a press release because it would have two apostrophes ("Center'd's new product . . ."). The apostrophe is also what's known as a "special character" in computer code, and it broke many features that we tried to build. Not only was the improper spelling a bad idea, but the name was also still unclear, so people did not know what we did or what we stood for. Really horrible decision all around. And one I would learn to correct in our final iteration of the product.

We had a vision of a world where people's lives were rooted in their local neighborhoods, making their connections with their neighbors stronger and their lives more convenient. Although that vision was clear, it took numerous efforts to launch something that has what entrepreneurs and investors call "product/market fit." This term means that you find a "good" (large and high-growth) market and have a product that can satisfy the needs of that market. We built three different products before ultimately finding one that had real product/market fit.

First up was Fatdoor, the neighborhood social networking product the team had built before I arrived. It had strong potential but was likely ahead of its time, as many tech products often are. When it was launched in 2007, it predated many of the foundational products upon which something like this would grow today, such as iPhone and Android apps, Facebook Connect (which allows people to log in to other sites with their Facebook credentials and carry their social graph with them), and other tools. So although the market was potentially large (all people wanting to connect in all neighborhoods), we had trouble reaching enough people in that market, which meant we couldn't effectively connect people locally. It also had some issues with user data privacy. So we shut it down. Round 1: failure.

Then came Center'd, version 1. The first version of Center'd we launched aimed to leverage what we built at Fatdoor, connecting people in neighborhoods, and focus on a specific community within those neighborhoods: schools and parents. The product helped them organize around work that needed to be shared and distributed, like event planning and volunteering, to help make their lives more convenient. It also had built-in virality, because each person who used the tool automatically pulled in more people. While the potential for a big market of people was there, a critical enough user need wasn't clear, so it wasn't a high-growth market. We ended up selling off the pieces of this to another small startup. Round 2: failure.

In Center'd 2.0, we built on top of the location-based work we had done in the first two products to extend into local search. We believed that the world was going mobile; when people looked for local businesses, they would want to quickly discover key attributes without reading hundreds of reviews on their smartphones (especially when most places averaged about four stars anyway). To build in that convenience, we analyzed more than 40 million online reviews for local businesses and used sentiment analysis and machine learning to come up with summaries for businesses, similar to a Zagat score, but in an automated way. We could tell you whether a restaurant was romantic, or kid friendly, or good for groups. We could let you know the most commonly mentioned menu items, what people said about the service, and how clean the bathrooms were. It was a really good product, but we couldn't get enough consumers to use it, and we had no real business model to make money to market it with because we couldn't sell ads in it unless people used it. Chicken and egg. We did find a set of customers who were really interested in the data we had—other local directories and search companies—and they wanted to pay us for the data. So we sold it to them, and started making money. *Awesome!* Until we realized we had already sold it to most of the largest potential customers. Meaning that we didn't have a sufficiently large market. Round 3: better, but still likely a failure.

At each of these junctures, I could have called it quits. Many people might have. I often say in retrospect that the company failed three times, but we just didn't go home. When the U.S. banks were being referred to as "too big to fail" in 2008 and 2009, we called ourselves "too stubborn to fail." Many people might have returned the remaining capital to investors and called it a day. And while I certainly felt anxiety and plenty of self-doubt in that moment, I didn't want to give up. We knew we had the right team, that the vision to improve people's local lives was worthwhile, and that the underlying tech had real potential. I thought back to all the research I had done running local and marketplace businesses at Yahoo! and what people had told us they felt was missing. One of the consistent unmet needs we heard from people was that they wanted to know about sales and deals nearby. That was it, our eureka moment. We decided to build our fourth product—The Dealmap—which took all the robust data we had about local businesses and added a layer that showed which businesses were having a sale or special offer at the time. We launched The Dealmap right as the local deals ecosystem around Groupon was taking off, and because we were able to map both local, Groupon-style deals and sales from national brands (like Gap) to their local stores, we had a superior product. While any local deals service might have a dozen or so deals in each city on a given day, we would have thousands. This was an idea that became a movement—people were passionate about it because it not only made their lives in their neighborhoods more convenient but also helped them save money that then could be put toward other valuable things. And unlike its predecessors, The Dealmap tapped into consumers' universal desire to save money. The product took off like wildfire after we launched it, acquiring millions of users in the first year. Companies like Mastercard and Microsoft reached out to work with us. It was a lightbulb moment for me in terms of what product/market fit actually looked like.

To use a Silicon Valley term in the zeitgeist: we embraced the pivot rather than accepting failure. And it worked.

Even though we were able to ultimately find success, what I've highlighted so far is just an inkling of the challenges we faced along the way. It was quite a tall mountain to climb. While there were many sunny days, there were also plenty of cloudy ones. In fact, even after we had a product that worked, in a market that was large, it didn't mean there were no more obstacles. We were sued by patent trolls, had to navigate a board that was split between taking more funding and selling the company, and had to rescue our acquisition by Google after it nearly fell apart thirty-six hours before it was supposed to close (and after my whole team knew about it and was packed up in boxes).

At each of those moments I just thought to myself, "Okay, how can I take one more step up the mountain?" And one by one, we did solve each challenge. I negotiated additional agreements when necessary, and we changed the structure of the Google acquisition. We did what it took to make it work. I am reminded of one of my favorite quotes: Pat Summitt, the late, beloved women's basketball coach from the University of Tennessee and the former coach of Robin Roberts, is famous for saying, "Left foot, right foot, breathe." Just keep moving. Solve each challenge that comes up, and eventually success will be within your grasp.

FIND YOUR ALLIES

WHEN THE MOUNTAIN feels high, remember that you don't have to climb it by yourself. Even if you start out as a solitary voice fighting for change, the people you rally around to support your movement can help you tackle obstacles, too. That's what Olga Rybkovskaya did when she successfully petitioned the Russian Ministry of Health to change its laws that had previously prohibited family from visiting relatives in intensive care units. Many of the people who signed her petition shared their personal stories on Change.org, and Olga collected those moving and powerful narratives and used their voices to encourage other signers to do the same. Marshaling her supporters and shaping them into a group of volunteers, including lawyers and psychologists who could help draft new proposed guidelines and directives, would turn out to be the most powerful aspect of her campaign. "I realized that many people need legal assistance and that among my signers there were lawyers," she told me. "I published the update suggesting we start a group of lawyers. A group of thirty signers responded immediately to this ask. I started a closed group on Facebook, and within a few days, as a result of 'brainstorming,' the volunteer lawyers in the group created a full package of the important and useful documents. Now the group still exists and my signers are still in touch with one another."

• • •

AND AMANDA NGUYEN, whom we met earlier, was passionate about fighting for the rights of sexual abuse survivors, but she also realized she couldn't do it alone. The first step she took toward finding allies in her movement to get the law changed was small but extremely powerful. She sent an e-mail to everyone she knew—colleagues, friends, professors—"asking people to walk with me in a vision of changing the Massachusetts bill. I said, 'This is what I want to do. Will you stand with me and help me?'" Sharing her story wasn't easy, but she knew it was an important part of changing how we talk about sexual assault. "Rape is still stigmatic for the survivor. When I see my name and the word 'rape' next to it, it's not a good feeling," she told me. "But I also see and hear from people across America and across the world about how much this means to them and how much of a difference it's made in their lives. That's why I keep doing it and keep putting myself out there and being vulnerable and authentic to the story that I'm trying to tell, my story, and the fight that I'm trying to get others to see. At the end of the day, that's what's important."

And people did respond—everyone from lawyers to coders to comedians asked Amanda how they could help. When Amanda founded Rise, she mobilized the forces she needed to fight for change on state and national levels. One of the many extraordinary things about the people who work at Rise is that most of them are volunteers—offering their services and various forms of expertise for free to a cause and movement they believe in. "Rise is like the Uber of activism," she told me. "The Rise model of advocacy is a share economy of professional skills for making change. Do you want to change your country in your spare time? Well, we've done that. There's zero excuse for anybody who says, 'Oh, I just don't have the capacity to do something full-time.' We had economists and people who make a living doing financial projects on Wall Street, who work crazy hours, but when we needed them to calculate regression for certain districts of a member of Congress, they spent two hours and we were able to produce that memo for that member. Our greatest assets were people, their stories and their backgrounds, their different professional skills and talents."

She also found allies in others who were survivors of sexual assault. Amanda started a Change.org petition, and as more than 140,000 people signed and wrote their reasons for supporting her, many people shared their own stories of survival. In fact, Amanda later raised money on Change.org to fly more than twenty of these fellow survivors to D.C. to tell their stories in person to members of Congress. And as we saw in Chapter 4, Amanda and her allies won, passing the federal law in just seven months. While getting the federal law passed is an enormous step forward, it is still just partway up the mountain Amanda and her allies are climbing. Each state has different laws, and many of the rights are not protected in every state. So Amanda is taking the movement to each state now as well, and many more survivors are starting campaigns in their home states. As of this writing, this incredible volunteer team has already passed the Sexual Assault Survivors' Bill of Rights in twelve states over the past six months.

SURROUND YOURSELF WITH PEOPLE WHO HOLD YOU UP (AND ACCOUNTABLE)

PARTNERS ARE THE ultimate allies. Amy Norman and Stella Ma cofounded Little Passports in 2008 after meeting in their jobs as category managers at eBay. Becoming entrepreneurs wasn't something they initially planned to do, but they were passionate about making a difference and felt that their work didn't make enough of an impact. As Stella told me, "I had been frustrated with corporate America, with not feeling like my work was having enough impact on the world. I couldn't look back and see how I had changed anything for the better." So they set off together as cofounders and co-CEOs to build Little Passports with the mission to raise a generation of global citizens. Little Passports offers a range of subscription products that inspire kids ages three to twelve to learn about the world by sending them packages in the mail each month that teach them about a different country or topic. All of the subscriptions are sent by characters, essentially "pen pals," who are traveling the world.

More than nine years later, Little Passports is a successful, high-growth, profitable company (nearly doubling in size every year), adding new products and inspiring kids around the globe. But to reach this point, Stella and Amy faced enormous challenges. And I mean enormous—both professionally and personally—that they had to overcome. And having each other really helped. I have been a board member at Little Passports since 2009 and have witnessed their incredible determination firsthand.

"The weekend that we founded the company, my marriage fell apart unexpectedly," Amy told me. "And I was eight months pregnant with my second child. Then my dad got diagnosed with cancer, and he died within four months. So, there I was, this single mom with no salary. I had just lost my dad, who was one of my best support systems, and we were trying to get this company off the ground. We literally had just launched; we didn't have any capital raised yet. And it took a huge amount of commitment and perseverance to stick with it, and this utmost belief in ourselves."

Amy went on to explain that for her, the company has always represented a tremendous sense of hope that came out of what was the absolute worst period of her life, and how having Stella there as her co-CEO made an enormous difference: "Stella has absolutely been the support system for me during those times. That stabilizing voice. I remember her bringing me into her home for Thanksgiving when I had nowhere else to go. And those are just memories that you never forget. And so, our business friendship is completely intertwined with our personal friendship. And it's an amazing feeling, all this time later, to have made it work out."

Stella, in turn, told me about one of the many times when Amy was there to support her through a difficult challenge: "Amy and I started out as best friends, and have really endured through the years. She was there to support me when I gave birth prematurely to my younger son and he was in the hospital for close to three months shortly after we had launched the business. Amy was there to support me both professionally and personally. That was really critical."

This combination of the belief in their business, their belief in themselves, and *their belief in each other* was key to getting them through the many obstacles and moments that felt like they might lead to failure, and being able to turn them around. They have managed not only to survive these tremendous personal challenges but also to overcome many tough times in the business itself—times when they couldn't raise capital and were afraid they couldn't pay their employees, times when they were changing warehouses and one company threatened to not release their inventory to them—and they got through these challenges together.

They tackled each potential failure point one by one, supporting each other through those tough moments, knowing they had each other to count on when they needed it, and feeling responsible to do their best for each other. They broke down the work into the areas where they each had the most expertise, and they trusted each other to each run their own areas—for Amy it was marketing and financial management, and for Stella it was product development and operations. And the biggest decisions about how to evolve their strategy, whether to launch new products or whether to work with certain investors, etc., they made together. This partnership has strengthened the company and helped them navigate to ultimate success. Little Passports is now on track to do more than $30 million in revenue and is growing quickly. And they have built a movement of passionate fans who love their brand and subscribe to multiple new products as they launch them.

· · ·

IT MAY SOUND obvious, but this technique of surrounding yourselves with other people who both support you and will hold you accountable is hugely effective in many parts of our lives. In fact, research shows that the simple act of sharing your goals with someone else makes you more likely to achieve them. In a 2015 study, Dr. Gail Matthews at Dominican University of California recruited 267 people from a variety of backgrounds and industries and asked them to take various actions on business-related goals they hoped to accomplish within a four-week block. Participants were randomly assigned to one of five groups with varying levels of commitment, starting with just "thinking" about their goals and rating them on different dimensions, and then increasing in additional commitments by writing down the goals, by writing down the goals and the action commitments, by doing all of the above and sharing action commitments with a friend, and finally by doing all of those steps while also sending a weekly progress report to a friend. Examples of the specific goals ranged from writing a chapter of a book to listing and selling a house.

At the end of the study, participants were asked to rate their progress and the degree to which they had accomplished their goals. Matthews found that more than 70 percent of the participants who sent weekly updates to a friend and 62 percent of those who shared action commitments with a friend reported successful goal achievement (completely accomplishing their goal or were more than half-way there), compared with 35 percent of those who kept their goals to themselves without writing them down, and 43 percent of those who wrote down their goals but didn't share them with others.

There are many examples of people having more success in reaching their goals when they feel supported by and accountable to others, everything from quitting smoking to losing weight and more. Recently a few friends of mine set up their own "support and accountability" circle of sorts with the goal of getting back in shape. They each made a plan to exercise four times a week, every week. Immediately after their workouts, they would text the others with a line or two about what the workout was. The others often, but not always, would then respond with encouragement. For any week when they didn't reach their goal of four workouts, the penalty was an extra seventy-five burpees (squat plus push-up plus frog jump plus jump squat) the following week, which, just as it sounds, is no fun.

At the end of one year, they estimate that they each missed only three to four weeks out of the more than fifty weeks since they made the deal. Two of them are in the best shape of their lives, and one says he's "close." The constant text reminders have been incredibly helpful, and the micro-goals that are week-to-week focused and not monthly or annual helped lead to a regular cadence of exercise. Even when they are traveling or otherwise out of their regular routine, this system has helped to actively encourage them to make a plan to get their four workouts in, and it nearly always works. They didn't even need to be in the same location—in this case one was in New York, one was in California, and one was in Australia—they could support each other across continents. And as a bonus, they've become even better friends because they are in touch day to day.

As you consider how to maximize your chances of success, think about those people you can partner with closely, who will support and encourage you in the tough times, and to whom you will feel accountable, giving yourself that extra push to tackle the challenges you will face.

DO THE WORK

MANY TIMES, MOVEMENTS and new businesses succeed through the sheer force of hunkering down and doing the hard work that comes with navigating challenges and starting something big. Creating something from nothing takes sweat equity—it isn't easy, and we shouldn't expect it to be. And you often don't have the resources you think you need to be successful, which means everyone involved needs to work harder, do more, and get by by being scrappy. But the work is worth it, and the scrappiness is worth it, and honestly, most big businesses and movements all have these same humble beginnings and just wouldn't have been successful without them.

It's no coincidence that many of the biggest tech companies from HP to Google are known for beginning in garages; when I first started Breakthrough in Pittsburgh we had just two rooms to work out of as our office, one of which was a closet, which we lovingly called the "cloffice." I worked so late every day that first year that I always carried around a shopping list in my pocket because I could never get to the store, which closed at 9:00 p.m. (Not a great way to set a leadership example, I know, and I later learned to prioritize a bit better.) But the truth is, in those early days of starting something, you often just have to do the work. And sometimes, the better things go, the more work there is to do, at least until you can adjust to the scale.

Alli Webb and Michael Landau at Drybar saw this in the weeks before they opened their first retail store. At first the bookings trickled in—they'd get an e-mail every few hours and everyone would get excited. But everything changed when *DailyCandy* ran the feature about them. Suddenly, while they were all at lunch together, their phones started buzzing: appointment notifications were pouring in. A week later, with eight styling chairs but only five stylists, they would be, as Michael told me, "thrown to the wolves." They had completely underestimated the demand. In the early days it was almost comical—Michael and Alli and both of their spouses would be in the shop until two in the morning, trying to figure out their systems and get ready for the next day. "It was pandemonium. Even a couple of months in, Alli was in this back room trying to do payroll, and trying to plan her schedule, and there were stylists literally on top of her," Michael said. "So I rented a one-bedroom apartment just behind the shop in Brentwood. My wife and I lived in Orange County, so we would come up on Monday, spend the week there, and Alli would come over from the shop and use that apartment to hear herself think, and do payroll, and do the schedule." Gradually they started hiring people and eventually they got a real office.

Even Alli—who was not only helping to run the business but also working with customers, doing hair—was shocked by how hard it was to keep up: "I didn't hire a manager because we didn't know how big this thing was going to be," she told me. "I was doing blowout after blowout and helping to manage the shop. And we had promoted 'Pop-ins welcome' on all of our material, so people were constantly coming in and getting mad because we were just too busy for that. On top of everything, when we first opened in Brentwood we had a phone at the front desk, but we couldn't answer the phone because we were so busy, and it was so loud with all the blow-dryers and the music. We very quickly realized that if we answered the phone, we were giving everybody a bad experience: the person standing in front of us for sure, and the person on the phone could barely hear us. That's how we ended up in the call center business, which we didn't plan. It was like catching our breath and trying to figure everything out at the same time. We just didn't expect it to take off so quickly the way it did. We were all crying the first day; it was insane."

In the end, as Michael says, it all comes down to just getting the work done. "Do not let 'perfect' get in the way of progress. Everything that is involved in growing a business is so hard, but you have to just be able to plow down, and get shit done."

PUT OBSTACLES IN PERSPECTIVE

AS IS TRUE for many of us, it took a few dramatic events in my life to massively change my outlook and help me put other challenges in perspective. We've already talked about Emma's accident, which was one of those events, but the first seismic shift in perspective took place eight years earlier, when I was in my late twenties.

My husband, Len, and I met in Pittsburgh, where he is from and where I had moved to start the Breakthrough program. We got married about two years later, and shortly after our wedding we started business school together, where we enjoyed two wonderful years at Cornell.

I had started having regular, fairly serious headaches around that time, but being young and busy, I really didn't give them much thought except to assume that I might have some kind of chronic sinus infection, since the pain I experienced was almost always right behind my eyes. We were focused on school and on each other, and it was a great time in our lives. Len is almost ten years older than me, and since he was then in his midthirties, he was ready to start having kids. Although I was younger, I had always known that I wanted to be a mother, and for some reason I've always had a healthy sense of fear about taking life's possibilities for granted, so I agreed. We might as well start trying now, I said at only twenty-six, because you never know what might happen.

We started trying to get pregnant, unsuccessfully, during our second year of business school, and after graduation we moved to Palo Alto, both for jobs in tech in the very early days of the dotcom boom. I went to see a new doctor in Palo Alto to try to get to the bottom of what I thought were fertility problems. At my second appointment, my doctor said the results of my blood work had shown some unusual hormone levels, and she suggested I should have a brain MRI.

For some reason, I honestly didn't think about why she might have prescribed that test at the time; maybe it was because I was young and naive, or maybe because it wasn't yet common to search every detail of every possible ailment on the Internet. Either way, all I know is that I was really unprepared for the news that lay ahead.

A few days later my doctor called. I was at work, so I took the call in one of the only private spaces I could find at Yahoo!'s open-plan offices—a glass conference room. As soon as I picked up the phone, she said rather abruptly: "We got your MRI back. You have a brain tumor and you need to call a neurosurgeon right away."

A brain tumor? I completely lost it.

Thoughts were racing through my head, and I remember feeling so scared and so confused. "How will I find a neurosurgeon? Does the fact that she said I need to call them right away mean that I am dying?"

Everyone could see me crying through the glass as I tried to process the news. I remember thinking: "How am I going to get out of here? Who am I going to have to talk to on my way out of the office so that I can leave?" Knowing what I now knew, I couldn't imagine staying at work for the rest of the day, but I didn't want to leave, either, not wanting to shirk my responsibilities as I was so new in my job—I had started working there full-time only one month earlier after having interned the previous summer. I remember finding my manager and telling him what was going on and how he encouraged me to go home. Though I wasn't a manager yet, this experience gave me valuable perspective for when I did become one and later a leader of a company. The empathy and sense of calm that my manager had for me on that day meant so much to me, and I have tried to replicate his kindness in the years since when others I work with are going through challenging times.

The day I found out about my brain tumor, I went home to try to process the news, and over the course of the following week, I learned more about my diagnosis and what my treatment options were. I had (and still have) what's called a pituitary adenoma, a slow-growing tumor that is usually benign and, as it turns out, fairly common. At the time, though, neither of those mitigating factors made my situation any less scary to me. However, I was both extremely scared and quite grateful—while my tumor was large and the surgical procedure incredibly involved and complex, it wasn't cancer. As long as the surgery went well, it was likely that I'd be fine.

Suddenly, too, all those years of headaches made sense. And here I was, about to have complex surgery on my brain, a young married woman, with no children, at nearly the same age the same thing had happened to my mother—twenty-seven.

It turned out that I was extremely lucky because the man who was likely the world's best surgeon for this type of tumor just happened to be in San Francisco. In fact, this doctor, Charlie Wilson, had been featured just two months before my surgery in a *New Yorker* article about "physical genius" by Malcolm Gladwell, who likened him to the Yo-Yo Ma or Wayne Gretzky of neurosurgery.

My tumor was getting quite large, and it was right up against my optic nerve, so there really was no other choice than to have the surgery: without it, the tumor would continue to grow and could cause blindness and other problems. Once I agreed to it, the surgery was scheduled. I would have to wait four weeks for the earliest available date.

It was a very frightening several weeks waiting for the surgery. I was afraid of so many things. What if I woke up in the middle of the surgery? What if something went wrong and I wasn't the same person afterward in terms of my cognitive ability, or my sight, or worse? Despite these fears, it was also an enlightening time, helping to put my life in perspective. As someone who was used to being in control and not asking others for help, I realized that I did need help, and this was one of my first exposures to the power of vulnerability. I owe so much to the people who helped me through that time, my immediate family of course, and also people like my father's cousin's wife, who is the director of pediatric endocrinology at Columbia and helped me get a better understanding of the procedure and make sure I was talking to the right physicians. And people like my business school friend Judy, who came over to give me a massage the night before my surgery. I would never have thought of asking someone for that, but instinctively she just knew it would help, and it truly did, reminding me that human connection is so, so important.

But the biggest shift in perspective that comes with an experience like this is the realization that life may be shorter than you think, and how important it is to be grateful for all the time we do have together. Sometimes, on days that are hard, I think about the letters I wrote before my surgery to Len, and to my parents, and to my sisters, just in case something went wrong, and I realize that whatever problem or stress I'm facing now pales in comparison. Because at this exact moment, there are others going into surgery, getting news of the loss of a loved one, or facing other life-and-death moments. I was very lucky to come through this experience, and I know that not everyone is so lucky.

IT'S ABOUT THE STRUGGLE

SOMETIMES, THE VALUE is actually in the obstacles themselves. My daughters had an amazing math teacher in elementary school whose innovative approach to the subject also taught valuable lessons for life. Math, she said, wasn't about getting the right or wrong answer.

It was about "the struggle."

Learning how to keep going, even when things get tough, is the critical skill to master. As she pointed out, the world's best mathematicians often spend years working on solving a single complex problem. She was trying to teach the kids in her class not only the math skills they needed, but also that they could struggle through something and not give up. She would give them exercises specifically to push them on this point by setting rules like, "You can use a calculator, but you can't use the multiplication button." By challenging them in these unique ways, she hoped to get them to think creatively about solving difficult problems, and also to encourage them to fight for a solution even when it is hard.

How you approach obstacles and challenges—where you believe your stores of grit and resilience come from—may be related to your ultimate success.

According to Carol Dweck, Stanford University psychologist and author of *Mindset: The New Psychology of Success*, people with a fixed mind-set believe that their traits are just givens. They believe they were born with a certain amount of intelligence or potential and that talent alone—not hard work—is what determines success. People with a growth mind-set, on the other hand, believe their qualities can be developed through their dedication and effort. Whatever skills and talents they've been born with are just the starting points for them. They understand that no one great has ever accomplished great things without years of passionate practice and learning.

Most people, Dweck explains in a *Harvard Business Review* article, don't only adhere to one mind-set or the other. We usually have a combination of these beliefs that changes with time and experience but that powerfully affects our potential for achievement. When situations are difficult, things change. "Even if we correct these misconceptions, it's still not easy to attain a growth mindset. One reason why is we all have our own fixed-mindset triggers. When we face challenges, receive criticism, or fare poorly compared with others, we can easily fall into insecurity or defensiveness, a response that inhibits growth."

Leaders and companies are also affected by the kind of mind-set they adopt. As Dweck explains: "Organizations that embody a growth mindset encourage appropriate risk-taking, knowing that some risks won't work out. They reward employees for important and useful lessons learned, even if a project does not meet its original goals. They support collaboration across organizational boundaries rather than competition among employees or units. They are committed to the growth of every member, not just in words but in deeds, such as broadly available development and advancement opportunities. And they continually reinforce growth mindset values with concrete policies."

A 2016 study published in *Frontiers in Psychology* by Dave Collins, Aine MacNamara, and Neil McCarthy confirms that the way athletes approach adversity is also what separates world-class "super champions" from the "almost champions" who were talented but didn't make it to the highest levels. The study found that super champions had an "almost fanatical reaction to challenge." Super champions talked about "how setbacks, injury or deselection for example, were catalysts for their development rather than roadblocks." In contrast, the almost champions talked about how easily things came to them initially, and then blamed setbacks on external causes, became negative, or lost motivation. Although both types of athletes faced similar challenges, how they reacted to those challenges was distinct and made a significant impact on their ultimate level of success.

Mastering the struggle isn't always easy—not in math, not in sports, and not in life. But day after day, ordinary people overcome the odds and push through hard times to achieve great things. And knowing that the more resilience we bring to facing the obstacles in our paths the more successful we are likely to be, certainly helps along the way.

FUN!™

WHEN FACING MAJOR obstacles, it helps not only to see the obstacles as opportunities to grow but also to find people who are good in a crisis. There are people out there who thrive in times of crisis, and it's great to find those people and keep them close to you. They can be terrific not only at helping you manage these challenging moments but also at helping you grow this skill within yourself.

Benjamin Joffe-Walt ("BJW," bear-hugger extraordinaire), who was introduced in Chapter 6, is one of these people. Before joining Change.org, he was an award-winning journalist for the *Guardian* and the *Telegraph*, covering major news stories around the world, particularly in Africa, from the genocide in Darfur to Hutu refugees in Rwanda. He's been at the center of some pretty tough situations. When we first met I remember hearing some of these stories, which started with comments like, "When I was arrested for bringing medicine to Cuba . . ." or "When I got dysentery in the Sudan . . ." You know, just like the stories we all tell around the dinner table, right?

When BJW ran the Change.org communications team, he told

his team that one way to handle a difficult crisis situation is to distance yourself enough emotionally from the seriousness of it and instead to see it as "fun." Obviously this strategy wasn't meant to downplay the gravitas of the incident, but rather to focus people on finding a solution to the challenge and on recognizing what could be learned from working your way through the crisis. It was a coping mechanism to deal with the sometimes overwhelming pressures of the job in a way that brought people together. The team had a group chat they were all part of, and whenever one of them would face a crisis or challenge in their country—a particular petition that the press was critical of, or someone accusing us of having fake signatures, etc.—they would all reply to that person in the chat with an ironic "Fun!" It took the edge off for the person whose job it was to manage that particular crisis and let them know that the rest of the team was there to support them. The late, amazing Jake Brewer, who used to run external affairs for Change.org and then went to work in the White House before dying tragically in a cycling accident in 2015, was great at this, too. He approached every crisis ready to charge in and was open-minded to different approaches. He took "Fun!" and added a "™" suggesting that if our team got really good at this, they could own it, even making it our trademark to be really great at tackling any type of challenging situation. So no matter how hard it got, the answer was always, "Fun!™"

In late 2016 I spoke on a panel about crisis management at a *Fortune* conference, where I met Brooke Buchanan, who has led communications teams at Walmart, Theranos, and Whole Foods, among other companies. She described this so well: "For some reason I love running into the fire." And she explained how she sleeps with two phones near her bed, just in case something important should happen. You want to find people like Brooke, BJW, and Jake—people who are at their best in challenging moments and can teach others to rise to the challenge as well.

As we worked with the team through ups and downs at Change.org, BJW and I often used a maritime metaphor when we talked to people about why the ability to stay calm and adaptable in difficult situations is a critical leadership skill at all levels: *You don't learn to be an outstanding captain by taking your ship out in a lake; you have to navigate a storm to really test yourself.* Great leaders have to be able to lead through storms as well as calm waters, and it helps to have shipmates who get fired up by the storm.

• • •

UNDERSTANDING THAT CHANGE is a process comprising multiple steps and stages that bring you from an ideal vision of a desired future to a sometimes imperfect present, full of ever-changing obstacles, requires a willingness to see setbacks and failures as potentially transformative moments. Persevering and remaining hopeful in the face of obstacles and finding creative ways to use criticism to advance your cause are crucial skills that all movement starters and leaders can master. And when you're on the dark side of the mountain, they will help you keep climbing.

YOU NEVER KNOW
WHOM YOU MIGHT
INSPIRE

ONE OF MY favorite parts of interviewing people for this book was hearing the stories of who had inspired each of them to start their movements in the first place. Nearly all the petition starters I talked to told me that they were hugely affected by others who had started similar campaigns or taken different kinds of social action. The idea that someone else was working to make change happen helped them see that it was possible for them to try it, too. Surprisingly, most of them had never told the other person that he or she was a crucial source of inspiration. We may never know the things we say or do that inspire other people, but we should be aware that our actions may have a small, sometimes profound, impact on others. And that's a powerful thing.

. . .

TARYN BRUMFITT, AN Australian mother of three, had a personal epiphany after struggling with her own negative body image for many years. She had considered plastic surgery and rejected it because she thought it would set the wrong example for her daughter. She then tried rigorous diet and exercise, training and successfully becoming an elite bodybuilder, but she told me, "The lifestyle that I lived to have that perfect body felt very restrictive, and it wasn't really very joyful." Taryn realized she was actually happier in her

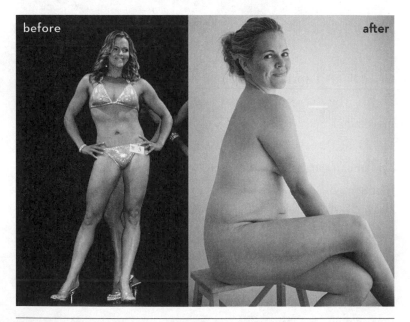

Taryn Brumfitt's before and after images
ANDRE AGNEW   KATE ELLIS

original body, one she now respected and loved more and treated with balance.

So she did something unexpected—she posted a "before and after" photo, with her chiseled bodybuilding body as the "before" image and her rounder, more balanced, joyful body as the "after" image.

Taryn didn't post the photo with the goal of inspiring others— she did it as part of her own journey of finding a way to love her body. And she had no idea just how many people that one image would inspire. It has now been viewed more than 100 million times, and more than 7,000 people reached out directly to Taryn through e-mail and social media to let her know just how inspirational she was to them. Her courage in posting that photo inspired tens of millions of people, led to her writing a book and producing a documentary, both called *Embrace*, and launching The Body Image Movement globally.

●　●　●

AMANDA NGUYEN, THE amazing young woman fighting for sexual assault survivors, shared a story with me about a surprising source of inspiration. After a particularly hard day lobbying in the Massachusetts State House, she went home and cried, feeling defeated and uncertain that she'd be able to convince career politicians to care about a cause they might not be personally familiar with. But the next day, when she took an Uber back to the U.S. Senate for another day of lobbying, her driver asked her why was going there. Amanda said, "I told him, and then this complete stranger started crying. His tears welled up from his eyes and he said, 'My daughter is a rape survivor, and when she tried to get help the system was so broken.' When he stopped the car he asked if he could shake my hand and thanked me for fighting for his daughter. Then he said, 'Has anyone told you that they love you today? I love you.' And I will never forget that father. One thing I've learned from this experience is that we might feel isolated when we're doing this work but it has ripple effects that are so powerful and so meaningful. And it's meaningful to people that you may not even know or think it impacts." Amanda had inspired this Uber driver, knowing that someone out there was fighting for his daughter. And in turn, he had inspired her. Simple words of appreciation meant so much to her, especially on that hard day.

• • •

SARA WOLFF, THE disability rights activist and motivational speaker with Down syndrome, was inspired by the people she met in the course of her duties supporting the ABLE Act. Talking to people and hearing their stories was the part of her role she found most meaningful and that kept her motivated to continue fighting for the rights of the disabled. "People inspire people because everybody can learn from each other," she told me. "I didn't know I was an advocate until high school when I learned that if I could stand up for myself, I knew I could do it for other people. I love it. Learning so much from people, hearing their stories about themselves, about their friends, their families, how they feel, is an amazing feeling."

Perhaps even more remarkable is how much Sara Wolff's activism inspired countless others in the disabled community and beyond. As National Down Syndrome Society (NDSS) president Sara Weir told me: "Sara Wolff is just nothing short of incredible. As she evolved and became the face of this legislation over the last decade, her ability to advocate and tell her personal story was something remarkable to watch. She grew as an advocate and as a person, by going through this journey. But probably something that most people didn't see is Sara's ability to set the bar high for that Mom or that Dad that had a baby born yesterday, or has a baby born tomorrow, with Down syndrome. They see Sara, and they see what she's been able to do. Testifying before the U.S. Senate finance committee, a person with Down syndrome—that doesn't happen every day. She set the bar really high. And she did it by just being who she is. She made people in the community with disabilities understand that the future is bright for people with Down syndrome. And they can achieve their own hopes, dreams, and passions."

• • •

WHEN I ASKED the people I interviewed who inspired them, I got answers as wide ranging as "my mom," to specific former colleagues and teachers, to "the punk band members I used to play with." Each movement starter could instantly name the people who had done small and large things to inspire them, yet only a few had told the source of their inspiration about the impact that person had made. Whether or not they had acknowledged the people who inspired them, each one has a crystal clear image of what made a difference—actions and words that showed them they could tackle huge problems and create the movements they went on to build.

While we certainly won't know all of the ways our actions affect others, we've seen that even the smallest gestures, like leaving a short comment—a "reason for signing"—on someone's petition can be a huge source of inspiration. Little things we say or write to people can do that, too. I can remember the positive, confidence-boosting impact of one professor who suggested I try to publish my final paper in an academic journal, and the corporate leader who took a chance on me and gave me a role that would be a stretch. And I have had the joy and surprise of being told by former students how my belief in them was a catalyst for their future success, and by people I've worked with that particular conversations we'd had in which I made a suggestion or gave some advice altered the shape of their career. We truly never know the effect we can have on other people.

When we shine a light on this, I hope it can push us toward doing two things:

1. *Think more about the impact we have on others.* Work to be kind and encouraging, to push people to new heights, both in big and small interactions. We never know whom our words and actions might inspire.
2. *Reach out to those who have inspired us to let them know they did.* Not only will it make our relationships stronger, but think about how much more positive the world would be if

we reinforced inspirational behavior by letting people know it worked—it just might cause people to do more of it.

Knowing whether we've had an impact on others is not the point. Living a life *in pursuit* of positive impact is what matters: a life of purpose, a life of service, and a life driven by hope. We've seen the power that can come from those who step up to start movements and from the large numbers of people who support them—new, purpose-driven companies, new ideas and approaches within staid organizations, and new policies and laws that create a better world for all of us.

Now it's your turn.

ACKNOWLEDGMENTS

In the spirit of "you never know whom you might inspire," there are countless people who have inspired me on the path to writing this book. First, my deepest gratitude goes to the profoundly inspiring people I was lucky to be able to interview for the book, including several whose incredible stories unfortunately did not end up in the final version, but whose courageous actions have made the world a better place and whose stories I will look for other opportunities to tell—Juliana Britto Schwartz and the Standing Rock Youth in North Dakota leading the movement against the Dakota Access Pipeline; Leah Busque, Task Rabbit founder and major contributor to the movement behind creating flexible work; Caroline De Haas of the movement to protect French labor laws; Consuelo Machado, who stood up for the educational rights of her son and other children with disabilities in Brazil; Richard Ratcliffe from the UK, who is fighting tirelessly for the release of his wife, Nazanin, imprisoned in Iran; and Shay Rubin, who while campaigning to get her health insurance company to cover cochlear implants for her young son successfully convinced the company to rewrite its policy to cover this procedure for all their customers who need it.

I want to thank my incredible colleagues from whom I have learned so much in the various stops along the route of my own career; so many of the examples from my life that are in the book would not have happened without the amazing people I worked alongside. Special thanks to Ben Rattray and my "frolleagues" from Change.org who opened my eyes to how people around the world are so bravely taking on the injustice they see, and taught me many of the techniques people use to do that. There are too many truly awesome colleagues to name from over the years; I hope you all know how much I appreciate you.

Acknowledging the people who have inspired me and whom I may have never properly told, I'm grateful for the many people in my life who have been mentors and coaches and have taken a chance on me, whether by challenging me, offering a job, investing in me (emotionally and/or financially), serving as a role model, recommending me for an opportunity, or simply believing in my potential: Jeanie and Jim Mohan, Barbara and Rob York, Beth Anderson, Chuck Lucasey, Doc Lamott, Joe DiPrisco, Peter Kuniholm, Tom Gilovich, John Brenner, the Potiguar family, Lois Loofbourrow, Mare (Kalin) Managan, Ham Clark, Marnie McKnight, Susan Dalton, Robert Frank, George Babbes, Karen Edwards, Grant Winfrey, Ken Grouf, Rob Solomon, Cammie Dunaway, Jeff Weiner, James Slavet, Hilary Schneider, Jerry Yang, Dave Goldberg, Bill Harris, Chandu Thota, Sergio Monsalve, Joe Hanauer, Susan Wojcicki, Sridhar Ramaswamy, Sameer Samat, Reid Hoffman, Arianna Huffington, Andrew Bosworth, Chris Cox, Kang-Xing Jin, Mark Zuckerberg, Sheryl Sandberg, Naomi Gleit, and many others. Having people in my life who believe in me and are willing to push me harder than I might push myself has been truly invaluable. It is their inspiration that I hope can pass through me to others via this book.

I want to thank Ed Faulkner, from Ebury, who heard the speech I gave in London in 2015 and approached me afterward to ask if I had ever considered writing a book. I'm not sure what he saw or heard that day that prompted him to suggest it, but I am immensely grateful, as this book would certainly not exist without him.

This book would also not exist without Laura Zigman, my writing partner in crime, who helped me through every stage of the process and every moment of self-doubt, leveraging her experience, talent, and witty sense of humor to keep me going. I am extremely grateful for her help and for all the time and enormous care she put into this book. And I want to thank Eva Arevuo and Callie Thompson for their help with so many parts of this process, from scheduling interviews to helping with research, to reading and commenting on early drafts of the book, as well as Shirl Harrison for her all-around support. Their help was so valuable along the way.

There are many people at Portfolio/Penguin to thank whose work has been critical to the final outcome. First, enormous thanks to my editor, Merry Sun. She was incredibly thoughtful and helpful in her suggestions and undoubtedly made the book significantly stronger in each round. I'm grateful for Portfolio publisher Adrian Zackheim, who had a clear initial vision for the book, encouraged me to think more broadly about the definition of movements, and helped bridge different perspectives to get alignment on where we wanted to take this. And I want to thank Stephanie Frerich, whose initial excitement about the book helped create early momentum and get us started in the right direction. I'm also grateful for the beautiful, creative work of art director Chris Sergio and interior designers Daniel Lagin and Tiffany Estreicher; the marketing team of Will Weisser, Katherine Valentino, Taylor Edwards, and Madeline Montgomery; publicity support from Alie Coolidge, Kelsey Odorczyk, and Tara Gilbride; production editor Sharon Gonzalez, managing editor Lisa D'Agostino, and the meticulous work of copy editor Angelina Krahn. (As a person who loves grammar, I secretly imagine another life as a copy editor, though clearly they do so much more than that.) Additional thanks to Lucy Oates, from Ebury, for spearheading the book in the UK and her feedback with an eye to the British audience.

Saving the most important people in my life for the big finale, I want to share the deepest gratitude for my parents, Bob and Judy Huret, my sisters, Deborah Op den Kamp and Bonnie Morrison, my closest friends, including "the gang of seven," my in-laws, the Dulski family, and Frans Op den Kamp, all of whom have given me unconditional love and support and truly immeasurable gifts, including so many of the lessons that appear in the book. And to my daughters, Emma and Rachel, and my husband, Len, I just simply could not have done this without you. I am so incredibly lucky that you are in my life and grateful that I am in yours. You give me purpose and you are the reason behind any movement I'm a part of.

NOTES

CHAPTER 1: BE PURPOSEFUL

1 **"Anyone who thinks that they are too small"**: Christine Todd Whitman, paraphrasing a quote attributed to the Dalai Lama.

6 **Nike highlights on its website:** The Nike Pro Hijab web, November 19, 2017, http://www.nike.com/ae/en_gb/c/women/nike-pro-hijab.

8 **Plum was the only wholly-owned subsidiary:** "B Corporation." Plum Organics | B Corporation. June 01, 2008. Accessed November 16, 2017, https://www.bcorporation.net/community/plum-organics.

8 **76 percent of the total baby food market by 2020:** Sandler Research, "Organic Baby Food Market—11.51% CAGR to 2020 Driven by EMEA," PR Newswire, July 7, 2016, http://www.sandlerresearch .org/global-organic-baby-food-market-2016-2020.html and https:// www.marketwatch.com/story/organic-baby-food-market—1151 -cagr-to-2020-driven-by-emea-2016-07-07-4203226.

9 **After creating that first set of bras:** Brielle Schaeffer, "Student Finds Niche in Bra World," *Jackson Hole News & Guide*, March 26, 2014, http://www.jhnewsandguide.com/news/business/student -finds-niche-in-bra-world/article_8569c52c-6c14-5b2b-a9ac -3012c13f73e9.html.

11 **"One of my absolute favorite things":** Elana Lyn Gross, "How Yellowberry Is Changing the Bra Industry for Pre-Teens," *Forbes*, April 17, 2017, http://www.forbes.com/sites/elanagross/2017/04/17/how-yellowberry-is-changing-the-bra-industry-for-pre-teens/2/.

14 **"Change doesn't happen inside the halls of power":** Manuela Bárcenas, "Sara El-Amine Shares Digital Advocacy Experience at Ottawa Progressive Policy Conference," *The Capital Times* (blog), March 31, 2016, http://ottcapitaltimes.wordpress.com/2016/03/31/sara-el-amine-shares-digital-advocacy-experience-at-ottawa-progressive-policy-conference/.

15 **A landmark study from 1966:** J. L. Freedman and S. C. Fraser, "Compliance Without Pressure: The Foot-in-the-Door Technique," *Journal of Personality and Social Psychology* 4, no. 2 (1966), 195–202.

17 **According to John Kotter and James Heskett:** John P. Kotter and James L. Heskett, *Corporate Culture and Performance* (New York: The Free Press, 1992).

17 *The Business Case for Purpose,* **a report:** Harvard Business Review Analytic Services and EY Beacon Institute, *The Business Case for Purpose* (Harvard Business School Publishing, 2015), http://www.ey.com/Publication/vwLUAssets/ey-the-business-case-for-purpose/$FILE/ey-the-business-case-for-purpose.pdf.

17 **64 percent of consumers say that a company's values:** Karen Freeman, Patrick Spenner, and Anna Bird, "Three Myths about What Customers Want," *Harvard Business Review*, May 23, 2012, http://hbr.org/2012/05/three-myths-about-customer-eng.

17 **"Now, more and more professionals look for positions":** Reid Hoffman, "The Power of Purpose at Work," ReidHoffman.org, November 6, 2015, http://www.reidhoffman.org/article/1470.

CHAPTER 2: SPARK A STANDING OVATION

21 **"The doing is the thing":** Amy Poehler, *Yes Please* (New York: Dey Street Books/William Morrow Publishers, 2014).

23 **Historian David Carter's research showed:** Gloria Teal, "The Spark That Lit the Gay Rights Movement, Four Decades Later," PBS.org, June 30, 2010, http://www.pbs.org/wnet/need-to-know/culture/the-spark-that-lit-the-gay-rights-movement-four-decades-later/1873/.

24 **And the Americans with Disabilities Act of 1990 was successful:** Arlene Mayerson, "The History of the Americans with Disabilities Act: A Movement Perspective," Disability Rights Education and Defense Fund, 1992, https://dredf.org/news/publications/the-history-of-the-ada/.

24 **"Change itself goes from the unthinkable":** Tiffany Shlain, "50/50: Rethinking the Past, Present & Future of Women + Power," (film), 2016, http://www.letitripple.org/films/50-50/.

28 **Research has shown that women are actually better:** Chiyoko Kobayashi Frank, Simon Baron-Cohen, and Barbara L. Ganzel, "Sex Differences in the Neural Basis of False-Belief and Pragmatic Language Comprehension," *NeuroImage* 105 (January 15, 2015): 300–11, doi:10.1016/j.neuroimage.2014.09.041; Gijsbert Stoet, Daryl B. O'Connor, Mark Conner, and Keith R. Laws, "Are Women Better Than Men at Multi-Tasking?" *BMC Psychology* 1, no. 18 (October 24, 2013), http://doi.org/10.1186/2050-7283-1-18; Danny Cohen-Zada, Alex Krumer, Mosi Rosenboim, and Offer Moshe Shapir, "Choking Under Pressure and Gender: Evidence from Professional Tennis," *Journal of Economic Psychology* 61 (August 2017): 176–90, https://doi.org/10.1016/j.joep.2017.04.005.

CHAPTER 3: BREATHE LIFE INTO YOUR VISION

51 **"Without vision":** Ken Auletta, *Googled: The End of the World as We Know It* (New York: Penguin Books, 2010).

55 **Marshall Ganz, a senior lecturer:** Marshall Ganz. "What Is Public Narrative: Self, Us & Now, 2009." (Public Narrative Worksheet). Working Paper. http://nrs.harvard.edu/urn-3:HUL.InstRe

pos:30760283 and https://dash.harvard.edu/bitstream/handle/1
/30760283/Public-Narrative-Worksheet-Fall-2013-.pdf?sequence=1

62 **"And the misconception is that a doctor":** "His Parents' Death Gave
Him a Mission: The Medical Brain Drain in Sub-Saharan Africa."
Goats and Soda: Stories of Life in a Changing World, National Public
Radio, April 28, 2017, http://www.npr.org/sections/goatsandsoda
/2017/04/28/525756657/his-parents-death-gave-him-a-mission-stop
-the-medical-brain-drain.

65 **The chart that follows is from the Center for Theory of Change:**
"Guided Example: Project Superwomen," Center for Theory of
Change, December 27, 2004, http://www.theoryofchange.org/pdf/
Superwomen_Example.pdf.

67 **In his TED talk about starting movements:** Derek Sivers, "How
to Start a Movement," filmed February 2010 at TED2010, TED
video, 3:09, https://www.ted.com/talks/derek_sivers_how_to
_start_a_movement.

68 **Alli Webb's first loyal clients:** "Blowing Hot Air," *DailyCandy*, February 10, 2010, http://www.dailycandy.com/los-angeles/article
/80153/Drybar-Blow-Dry-Studio-Opens.

68 **The statistics show just how persuasive influencers are:** "Nielsen:
Global Consumers' Trust in 'Earned' Advertising Grows in Importance," news release, April 10, 2012, http://www.nielsen.com/us/en
/press-room/2012/nielsen-global-consumers-trust-in-earned
-advertising-grows.html.

70 **As Gretta described in an interview with *Influencive*:** Jenny Gao,
"How to Make $1M in a Day with Gretta van Riel, Instagram Queen,"
Influencive, June 22, 2017, http://www.influencive.com/gretta-van-riel.

70 **In a recent interview with *Foundr*:** Nathan Chan, "How Gretta
Rose van Riel Built Multiple Multimillion Dollar Ecommerce Businesses with This One Simple Hack," *Foundr*, May 25, 2017, http://
foundrmag.com/gretta-rose-van-riel-influencer-marketing/.

71 **"The North Star of any campaign"**: Esha Chhabra, "Meet the Female Entrepreneur Who Raised Over $3 Million from Crowdfunding, Not VCs," *Forbes*, July 31, 2017, http://www.forbes.com/sites /eshachhabra/2017/07/31/meet-the-female-entrepreneur-who -raised-over-3-million-from-crowdfunding-not-vcs/.

CHAPTER 4: GET TO KNOW GOLIATH

77 **"Don't raise your voice"**: "Don't Raise Your Voice—Improve Your Argument," *Murmurings to the Masses* (blog), November 24, 2004, http://people.cs.uchicago.edu/~srasul/blog-archives/murmur-v1 /C1092540138/E714722103/index.html.

81 **"Nonviolence seeks to defeat injustice"**: "The King Philosophy," The Martin Luther King, Jr. Center for Nonviolent Social Change, http://www.thekingcenter.org/king-philosophy.

81 *New Yorker* **writer Malcolm Gladwell suggests**: Malcolm Gladwell, *David and Goliath: Underdogs, Misfits, and the Art of Battling Giants* (New York: Little, Brown and Company, 2013).

82 **"What the Israelites saw"**: Gladwell, *David and Goliath*.

87 **"I want the EU to impose further sanctions"**: Reuters, "Brown Calls for More EU Sanctions on Myanmar," October 6, 2007, http:// www.reuters.com/article/us-myanmar-britain-idUSL06416574 20071006.

95 **Lia and Tessa started by filming their own documentary**: Tessa Hill and Lia Valente, "'Allegedly,' the Rape Culture Doc by Grade 8 Consent Activists," *Huffington Post Canada*, June 23, 2015, http:// www.huffingtonpost.ca/2015/06/23/allegedly-rape-culture-tessa -hill-lia-valente_n_7637832.html.

109 **"The existential battle they had been so desperately fighting"**: Benjamin Wallace, "SeaWorld, Breached," *New York*, May 4, 2016, http://nymag.com/daily/intelligencer/2016/04/seaworld-tilikum -orcas.html.

112 **"We know members have requested a blocking feature":** Paul Rockwell, "Protect Your Users From Stalkers and Help Keep Victims Safe," (blog), Change.org, February 21, 2014, https://www.change.org/p/linkedin-protect-your-users-from-stalkers-and-help-keep-victims-safe/responses/10562.

CHAPTER 5: LEAD YOUR CREW

117 **"Contrary to what I believed as a little girl":** Tina Fey, *Bossypants* (New York: Little, Brown and Co. 2011).

125 **Özgecan Aslan, a nineteen-year-old Turkish university student:** RT, "Massive Protests in Turkey after Student Murdered and Burnt in Attempted Rape," RT.com, February 14, 2015, http://www.rt.com/news/232423-turkey-protests-student-rape/.

126 **"crimes against women are part of our everyday":** "The Six People You've Never Heard of Who Changed the World in 2015," *Independent*, December 31, 2015, http://www.independent.co.uk/voices/the-six-people-youve-never-heard-of-who-changed-the-world-in-2015-a6792246.html.

131 **Wharton professor and bestselling author Adam Grant:** A. M. Grant, E. M. Campbell, G. Chen, K. Cottone, D. Lapedis, and K. Lee, "Impact and the Art of Motivation Maintenance: The Effects of Contact with Beneficiaries on Persistence Behavior, *Organizational Behavior and Human Decision Processes* 103 (2007), 53–67.

131 **When callers were able to speak:** Susan Dominus, "Is Giving the Secret to Getting Ahead?," *New York Times Magazine*, March 27, 2013. http://www.nytimes.com/2013/03/31/magazine/is-giving-the-secret-to-getting-ahead.html.

133 **The effect was first demonstrated in 1966:** Robert Rosenthal and Lenore Jacobsen, *Pygmalion in the Classroom: Teacher Expectation and Pupils' Intellectual Development* (New York: Holt, Rinehart and Winston, 1968).

133 **The teachers' high expectations of those students:** John Rutkie-wicz, "Great Expectations Drive Great Performance," Living As A Leader, https://www.livingasaleader.com/great-expectations.

133 **As Zenger and Folkman describe:** Jack Zenger and Joseph Folk-man, "If Your Boss Thinks You're Awesome, You Will Become More Awesome," *Harvard Business Review*, January 27, 2015, http://hbr.org/2015/01/if-your-boss-thinks-youre-awesome-you-will-become-more-awesome.

142 **Research by Alison Wood Brooks and Francesca Gino:** Alison Wood Brooks and Francesca Gino, "Asking Advice Makes a Good Impression," *Scientific American*, March 1, 2015, http://www.scientificameri can.com/article/asking-advice-makes-a-good-impression1/.

146 **Recent data from a two-year study:** Julia Rozovsky, "The Five Keys to a Successful Google Team," *re:Work* (blog), November 17, 2015, http://rework.withgoogle.com/blog/five-keys-to-a-successful-google-team/.

151 **It's an idea championed by experts like Brené Brown:** Brené Brown, "The Power of Vulnerability," filmed June 2010 at TEDx-Houston, TED video, 20:19, http://www.ted.com/talks/brene _brown_on_vulnerability.

152 **health benefits covered in the Zadroga Act:** Jessica Glenza, "Con-gress Passes Bill to Extend Health Coverage for 9/11 Responders," *Guardian*, December 16, 2015, http://www.theguardian.com /us-news/2015/dec/16/congress-spending-bill-budget-zadroga-911 -health-and-compensation-act.

154 **"In Mississippi, where I'm from":** Robin Roberts with Veronica Chambers, *Everybody's Got Something* (New York: Grand Central Publishing, 2014).

155 **"I remember . . . when I was unfortunately diagnosed with breast cancer":** Robin Roberts, interview by Rachel Martin, "Wise Words from Robin Roberts' Mom: 'Honey, Everybody's Got Something,'" *Weekend Edition Sunday*, NPR, April 27, 2014, http://www.npr.org

/2014/04/27/306542402/wise-words-from-robin-roberts-mom
-honey-everybody-s-got-something.

159 **the Fundamental Attribution Error:** Lee Ross and Leonard Berkowitz, "The Intuitive Psychologist and His Shortcomings: Distortions in the Attribution Process," in *Advances in Experimental Social Psychology*, vol. 10 (New York: Academic Press, 1977), 173–220.

160 **Brené Brown refers to it as the "hypothesis of generosity":** Brené Brown, *Rising Strong: The Reckoning. The Rumble. The Revolution* (New York: Spiegel & Grau, 2015).

160 **My friend Kate Gamble Dickman wrote one of the most beautiful posts:** Kate Gamble Dickman, "Beam Me Up, Sweet Scotty," January 9, 2017, http://medium.com/@kategambledickman/beam
-me-up-sweet-scotty-fab26b8b6ab9.

164 **If you read the *Urban Dictionary* entry for coxswain:** Urban Dictionary (web), definition by Portpressure, July 01, 2005, https://www.urbandictionary.com/define.php?term=coxswain.

165 **an increasing amount of research shows that humor:** Alan W. Gray, Brian Parkinson, and Robin I. Dunbar, "Laughter's Influence on the Intimacy of Self-Disclosure," *Human Nature* 26, no. 1 (March 2015), https://doi.org/10.1007/s12110-015-9225-8.

165 **In fact, some business schools are offering classes in humor:** Joel Stein, "Humor Is Serious Business," *Insights by Stanford Business*, July 11, 2017, http://www.gsb.stanford.edu/insights/humor-serious
-business.

CHAPTER 6: DON'T DRINK THE HATERADE

167 **"Don't feed the trolls":** Scott Stratten, *UnMarketing: Stop Marketing. Start Engaging* (Hoboken, NJ: John Wiley & Sons, 2012).

170 **"If you absolutely can't tolerate critics":** Xeni Jardin, "What Amazon's Jeff Bezos Thinks about Peter Thiel and Hulk Hogan vs. Gawker," June 1, 2016. https://boingboing.net/2016/06/01/what

-amazons-jeff-bezos-thin.html. Link to video: https://www.youtube .com/watch?time_continue=291&v=Mf0e8M5Fxfo (4:51).

170 **Research shows that the amygdala:** "Understanding the Stress Response," Harvard Health Publishing, March 2011, updated March 18, 2016, https://www.health.harvard.edu/staying-healthy /understanding-the-stress-response; Tiffany A. Ito, Jeff T. Larsen, N. Kyle Smith, and John T. Cacioppo, "Negative Information Weighs More Heavily on the Brain: The Negativity Bias in Evaluative Categorizations," *Journal of Personality and Social Psychology* 75, no. 4 (1998), 887–900, http://dx.doi.org/10.1037/0022-3514.75.4.887.

171 **When *New York Times* writer Tony Schwartz did this:** Tony Schwartz, "Overcoming Your Negativity Bias," *Dealbook* (blog), *New York Times*, June 14, 2013, http://dealbook.nytimes.com/2013/06/14 /overcoming-your-negativity-bias/.

175 **"Hasbro . . . would only feature girls on the boxes":** McKenna Pope, "McKenna Pope: Want to Be an Activist? Start with Your Toys," filmed November 2013 at TEDYouth 2013, TED video, 5:22, http://www.ted.com/talks/mckenna_pope_want_to_be_an_activist _start_with_your_toys.

175 **"It was like *Willy Wonka and the Chocolate Factory*":** McKenna Pope, "McKenna Pope: Want to Be an Activist? Start with Your Toys," filmed November 2013 at TEDYouth 2013, TED video, 5:22, http://www.ted.com/talks/mckenna_pope_want_to_be_an_activ ist_start_with_your_toys.

183 **There is a classic example of the Bear Hug:** "A Victim Treats His Mugger Right," *Morning Edition*, NPR, March 28, 2008, http://www .npr.org/2008/03/28/89164759/a-victim-treats-his-mugger-right.

186 **"No one is born hating another person":** Nelson Mandela, *Long Walk to Freedom* (New York: Little, Brown and Company, 1994).

187 **"Matthew decided his best chance":** Eli Saslow, "The White Flight of Derek Black," *Washington Post*, October 15, 2016, http://www

.washingtonpost.com/national/the-white-flight-of-derek-black /2016/10/15/ed5f906a-8f3b-11e6-a6a3-d50061aa9fae_story.html.

189 **"Several years ago, I began attending a liberal college":** R. Derek Black, "Why I Left White Nationalism," *New York Times*, November 26, 2016, http://www.nytimes.com/2016/11/26/opinion/sunday /why-i-left-white-nationalism.html.

CHAPTER 7: MOUNTAIN CLIMBING

195 **This thing we call "failure" is not the falling down:** Mary Pickford, *Why Not Try God?* (Culver City: Northern Road Productions, 2013). First published 1934 by H. C. Kinsey & Co.

199 **Ben Silbermann, the founder and CEO of Pinterest:** "Ben Silbermann Keynote Address at Alt Summit," Vimeo video, 1:05:38, filmed January 27, 2012, in Salt Lake City, http://vimeo.com /user10165343/review/35759983/820bd84fa4.

202 **"But as F. Scott Fitzgerald wrote":** F. Scott Fitzgerald, *Tender Is the Night* (New York, Charles Scribner & Sons, 1934).

202 **"It ain't about how hard you hit":** "*Rocky Balboa* (2006) Quotes," IMDb, http://www.imdb.com/title/tt0479143/quotes.

203 **The speed of getting through failures:** Gerald Beals June. The Biography of Thomas Edison (web). 1999. http://www.thomasedison .com/biography.html.

204 **"I was more likely to report seeing a UFO":** Amram Shapiro, Louise Firth Campbell, and Rosalind Wright. *The Book of Odds: From Lightning Strikes to Love at First Sight, the Odds of Everyday Life* (New York: William Morrow, 2014).

210 **"Left foot, right foot, breathe":** "Pat Summitt's Son: 'God Has Bigger Plan for Her,'" CBS News, April 20, 2012, http://www.cbsnews .com/news/pat-summitts-son-god-has-bigger-plan-for-her/.

216 **In a 2015 study, Dr. Gail Matthews:** "Study Focuses on Strategies for Achieving Goals, Resolutions," Dominican University of Califor-

nia, http://www.dominican.edu/dominicannews/study-highlights
-strategies-for-achieving-goals.

224 **In fact, this doctor, Charlie Wilson, had been featured:** Malcolm
Gladwell, "The Physical Genius," *New Yorker*, August 2 1999, http://
www.newyorker.com/magazine/1999/08/02/the-physical
-genius.

226 **According to Carol Dweck:** Carol Dweck, "What Having a 'Growth
Mindset' Actually Means," *Harvard Business Review*, January 13,
2016, http://hbr.org/2016/01/what-having-a-growth-mindset
-actually-means.

226 **"When we face challenges":** Dweck, "What Having a 'Growth
Mindset' Actually Means."

227 **As Dweck explains:** Dweck, "What Having a 'Growth Mindset' Actually Means."

227 **A 2016 study published in *Frontiers in Psychology*:** Dave Collins,
Aine MacNamara, and Neil McCarthy, "Super Champions, Champions, and Almosts: Important Differences and Commonalities on
the Rocky Road," *Frontiers in Psychology*, January 11, 2016, http://
journal.frontiersin.org/article/10.3389/fpsyg.2015.02009/full.

INDEX

INDEX

INDEX